ASPECTS OF
RURAL ESTATE MANAGEMENT

Aspects of
Rural Estate Management

by

Professor C.W.N. Miles C.B.E., M.A., F.R.I.C.S.
H.A.R. Long B.A., F.R.I.C.S.
and
Professor W. Seabrooke B.Sc., PhD., F.R.I.C.S

1995

A member of Reed Business Publishing

The Estates Gazette Limited
151 Wardour Street, London W1V 4BN

First published 1995
ISBN 0 7282 0254 9

Typesetting by Amy Boyle Word Processing, Rochester, Kent
Printed by Bell and Bain Ltd., Glasgow

This was one of my prayers: for a parcel of land, not so very large, which should have a garden and a spring of ever-flowing water near the house, and a bit of woodland as well as these.

Horace

Preface

It may at first seem that the individual chapters of this book are not related to one another, but this is not so. If they are looked at one at a time they are similar to the random pieces of a jigsaw puzzle, but when put together they do show something of a pattern; at least so the authors hope.

The ownership of land is a legal fiction; this point is made clearly in the first two chapters, which deal with the nature of property rights, show briefly how they evolved and how and by whom they may be exercised. It is essential to distinguish between the full ownership of these rights (which are always capable of being overridden by action of the State) and temporary or limited ownership. The latter is usually made visible by occupation, which is the only evidence of ownership apparent to the casual observer. Of course the freehold owner may also be in occupation, and often is, but it is in most cases occupation which draws attention to ownership.

So, ownership is upheld by law long established; but what brought this about? It is suggested that the need to establish and defend territory is one of mankind's animal instincts, that attachment to territory, be it permanent or temporary, is embedded in most of us and that those with no territory wander forlorn. While the extent of the territory we occupy is of small moment (for it is occupation not ownership which matters) in human terms, the territorial imperative has been exploited and the establishment of status has demanded that the larger the unit of ownership the more highly respected, in all sorts of ways, the owner should be. Today sheer wealth has largely taken over as the yardstick of social esteem, but wealth without land may be hidden (indeed it sometimes is) whereas land as wealth, however real or imagined, is evident and carries with it responsibilities apparent to all. The ownership of land gave power and to some degree it still does so. It was this power, local and national, which was sought over the centuries by the acquisition of land; but this is a subject of separate study, not of this book.

We are where we are and, however acquired, land has to be

managed; peopled as it is and used as it is and abused as it may be. This book looks at some of the management problems of the landed estate, which, treated as a very particular asset, is ever in the public eye. Ownership of land is often viewed with envy and sometimes with the conviction that it should be in the public domain. If it were, then the owner's responsibilities and powers would have been transferred from individual to official, leaving the "public", the man on the Clapham Omnibus, much where he was before.

It must be acknowledged, perhaps with mixed feelings, that there are organisations or bodies, some officially constituted some not, which claim the right to interfere with or direct certain of the privileges and processes of land ownership and management. It is within the obligations of management to consider the impact and power of these bodies and indeed how far they should be taken seriously.

What then is management? The use of resources "to the best advantage"; but of whom? Without prudent financial management the best use is not attainable and in the process of such management it is wise to examine the resources, to consider, even if only by questions to which an answer is not at once forthcoming, the basis of value of both capital and income. The process of management can only be directed if those involved in it know or have some idea of what it is they should be trying to achieve. Objectives must, therefore, be set and progress monitored.

The institutional landowner may be able to set and keep to long-term objectives without frequently digging up the plant to see how it is growing; the private owner may be unable to adhere to long term objectives, particularly if he is unsure for how long ownership within the family can be maintained; consequently, one objective may be so to structure and manage the estate that as much as possible of it is passed on to future generations. This objective is often impossible to achieve; but in management thought must be put to it. Possible solutions are many: some may involve the establishment of trusts of one kind or another, some may even demand the establishment of charitable land trusts under which ownership will pass from the family to a trust, whose main function is the preservation of the estate or a part of it. Such action will be altruistic by the owner or the family, but that it takes place at all does highlight the fact that the ownership of land in the form of an estate, particularly a country estate, is the ownership of something dear to many a heart, which in single ownership may be fashioned as a social entity, a group, indeed in primitive terms almost a tribe devoted to its defensible space and capable of living together as a community into which newcomers may be integrated, after a time.

This book seeks to deal with certain of the issues raised in this preface and with other matters of moment and interest to landowner and manager which have perhaps not been brought together before. Maybe the pattern of the puzzle which lay before the reader at first in pieces will by the end have become apparent.

In harmony with some of the thoughts expressed in this book, but perhaps also in some discord with them it may be appropriate to end with a quotation which gives the authors at any rate, some joy.

> They love their land because it is their own
> And scorn to give ought other reason why.
> Would shake hands with a king upon his throne
> And think it kindness to his majesty.
>
> Fitz-Green Halleck (1790–1858)

Contents

CHAPTER 1

The nature of property

Synopsis
Introduction – Property rights – Institutional nature of property rights – Power of property rights in land use decisions – Essential features of property – Ownership – Riparian rights – Possession – Proof of title – Transferability – Coastal zone – Tidal watercourses – Foreshore – Seabed.

Introduction

This chapter attempts to define and explain the significance of property rights as they have become defined by the English system of common law. It is not a summary of the law of real property, but attempts to define the rights and powers which users of land may exercise and some of the limits to those powers. The extent of the rights available to their owner determines to a very large degree the value of the "property" which those rights identify.

The human species has the capacity to conquer, exploit and destroy the natural environment and yet to appreciate and safeguard its intrinsic value. The opportunity to exercise the power of exploitation is sometimes considered as a basic "right". Taking advantage of such power may, however, create costs which have to be borne by other members of society, who do not share in the benefits. In an ordered society rights, powers, duties and responsibilities encompassing individual and collective aspirations are organised so that when these are not necessarily congruent, when they diverge or conflict, mechanisms of control and conflict resolution may be applied.

The development and use of natural resources in a manner which is proactive and forward-looking, which enables action and progress to occur and, above all, sustains the long-term value of those resources, requires an operating framework which maintains an appropriate balance between the dynamic impetus of development and the restraining influence of control. Property rights represent a powerful, legitimate source of authority when considering the allocation of natural resources. They are also a powerful source of conflict if private values conflict with social costs. The expression of such social costs or externalities typically arises from non-property rights. Such expressions become increasingly powerful as they become co-ordinated and organised. Powers arising from either source must, to be socially acceptable, be legitimised by the code of law which governs the operation of society and individuals and organisations within it.

Property rights

Society has evolved a system of "property rights" which enables these powers to be exercised in an orderly fashion, operating according to rules of definition and conduct which may be formal and explicit or informal and implicit. The system of property rights operates sometimes in harmony, sometimes in conflict with other institutions designed to facilitate the exchange or transfer of property rights; to control the effect of their utilisation on society at large; and to resolve conflicts arising from the exercise or neglect of property rights and other competing interests. The power and authority assu.iated with property rights relies either on imposition by force or on social acceptability. The normal standards of civilised behaviour dictate that social acceptability is preferable, but history is littered with examples of the imposition of property rights by the exercise of force.

The institutional nature of property rights

The first notable step in the institutionalisation of property rights in England was their establishment and consolidation in the common law by the Normans in the 11th and 12th centuries. The feudal structure which they introduced relied upon a direct association between the control of land and the ruling elite. The evolution of a mercantile and then industrial capitalist society occurred largely without the revolutionary upheaval experienced elsewhere. Land came to represent the more ubiquitous notion of wealth as well as privilege. The structure of property rights and the power associated with them remained largely intact, dominated by the requirements of the landed aristocracy.

Under these circumstances, the institutional framework within which the utilisation of land and natural resources occurred was largely preordained and highly deterministic. It was clear and unambiguous from the constitutional level of the ruling elite to the operational level of the landowner. Unsuppressed conflicts were resolved by mechanisms which were largely designed and controlled by the holders of property rights. Up to and beyond the end of the 19th century the landowning aristocracy not only maintained very direct control over the manner in which their estates were managed, but they also more or less controlled the economic, political and social institutions which determined the environment within which land utilisation occurred.

The power of property rights in land use decisions

The foundations of land and natural resource management have become fragmented and disconnected. The power of landowners has diminished and became fragmented, the demand for "rights" of use and access (particularly for relaxation and recreation) has become more manifest. At the constitutional level (legislature and executive) new institutions have emerged (eg quangos) and old institutions have evolved to meet new demands. The same has happened at the organisational level (eg local government). At the operational level, property rights themselves, as defined by English law, can be inflexible and unwieldy. Denied the support of constitutional and organisational authority, the traditional institutions of land management have become less effective in dealing with decisions relating to resource allocation, resource management and conflict resolution.

These are complex, interrelated issues, susceptible to the problems created by ambiguity and uncertainty, in particular, the constant adjustment and reappraisal of parameters and values. Isolating and prioritising "key" issues and conflicts requiring professional judgment has become difficult. The scope for error in making judgments on unreliable or ambiguous information is large. Property rights, particularly freehold ownership, are sometimes used to bludgeon a way through the tangle of interwoven complexities. This may be effective, but an inefficient way of solving relatively precise problems such as safeguarding an area of natural habitat. Modern landowners, denied the "shogunate" powers of past generations, are less able to absorb costs associated with resource allocation decisions or to contain the wider effects of such decisions.

The motivation to exercise the power to exploit the natural environment is strongly influenced by the perceived interaction between values and costs. It is correspondingly limited by uncertainty arising from shifting perceptions of what is possible and what is desirable. The possession of property rights constitutes the most powerful mechanism, other than military conquest, for enabling these perceptions to be acted upon. However, their significance varies according to the perceived value of the resources to which they relate and their accessibility. In most of the developed economies of the world the framework of property rights is relatively well developed. Even so, property rights may be ambiguous in inaccessible areas and become progressively more so in those parts of the natural environment to which the human species is less well suited for survival: most notably the sea and space.

Technological advances have permitted greater access to hitherto inaccessible regions of the earth's ecosystem. The evolution of civilisation may be characterised by an urge to explore and colonise uncharted parts of the earth and then to convert public space to "possessed" space. The value of the resources comprising newly accessible horizons has encouraged the adaptation of land-based institutions governing the ownership, possession, control and transferability of resources, in other words establishing property rights governing their use and exploitation.

The essential features of property

The term "property" has, up to this point, been used without definition. It is a common term but possesses several meanings, for example, an artefact on a stage; a characteristic of a person, place, substance, etc. In the context of "property rights", however, it has yet another meaning. Used in relation to land and buildings, for example, property is an inherently social concept providing a powerful motivating factor for much human behaviour. It has exercised the minds of philosophers, economists, politicians and, inevitably, lawyers. Lawyers, in particular, have played an important role in defining precisely what constitutes "property" and what rights and duties flow from it.

Three of the most salient features of property are *ownership*; *possession*; and *transferability*. Property is, then, the object to which rights of ownership, possession and transferability can legitimately be applied. Of these, the most critical and often most contentious are ownership and possession. In some senses they are associated with loss of freedom. Ownership of something which is self-sustaining, rather than something falling victim to the destructive effects of entropy is particularly prized and this, of course, applies to land and water above all other things. In the context of land, if not other forms of property, the entitlement to use and enjoy property is identified and expressed in the form of "rights"; indeed, property in this sense is sometimes referred to as an bundle of rights. It is an enabling concept, enabling members of society to use resources, either bestowed by nature or invented by society, in an orderly fashion.

Legal identification and recognition of these rights is the first stage in achieving this orderly utilisation. Initially, therefore, two of the most fundamental characteristics of property which require careful consideration are *ownership* and *possession*. Implementation and enforcement of processes of utilisation rely on additional mechanisms characteristically based on economic and political principles of resource allocation. This raises the third essential characteristic of property, namely the ability for its ownership to be *transferred* from one owner to another. Simple possession, even the right to possess, is just part of a more comprehensive right associated with "property".

English law distinguishes between *personal* property (any property other than land) and *real* property. The corresponding distinction in Scottish law is drawn between *heritable* (immovable) property and *movable* property. Personal property is divided into two main categories: choses in possession and choses in action. Choses in possession are things that can actually be possessed and transferred by physical delivery. Choses in action are not tangible physical objects. The owner's right to them cannot be asserted by taking possession, but only by means of an action. Choses in action include: negotiable instruments (written documents representing money); patents and designs; copyright, trade marks and trade names. Land is an inherently more complex type of property, categorised by lawyers as "real" property for reasons which are mediaeval in origin, but, essentially, property was classed as "real" if the courts would contemplate restoring possession to a dispossessed owner (as distinct from merely awarding compensation for the loss).

In the case of personal property, ownership and possession are invariably thought of as one and the same thing. In the case of real property they are quite distinct; an owner who is also in possession of the property is referred to as an "owner-occupier" to indicate the two characteristics in one. Common sense dictates that possession cannot necessarily be synonymous with ownership because land so manifestly lacks portability. Indeed, if it were portable it would not be land; the two things are mutually incompatible. At the same time, land cannot be hidden away and to be useful it is, in most cases, accessible. In the days when possession of land could be won by force of arms, sites which were inaccessible or easily defensible were valuable for that reason. In some respects, feudal society was based on military acquisition or possession of land and the subsequent military defence of landholdings. The history of landownership is littered with disputes about rightful ownership and the rights which ownership rightfully bestows.

Physical manifestation is ostensibly the most powerful, ubiquitous feature of the phenomenon we refer to as land and everything physically associated with it. There is nothing more real, tangible. It conjures up images of woods and fields; roads and buildings; countryside and coast; towns and villages. Traditionally change in the fabric of land and buildings is slow and measured. Features of the landscape or townscape are thought of as stable if not static. Indeed, this sense of stability in an otherwise changing world has been exploited by politicians and money-lenders to foster the belief that there is no better route to financial prudence and individual prosperity than to have a stake in this basic resource – no less than the fabric of the planet itself. However, technological progress has given man the power to effect radical change on the landscape by using machines of immense power; economic "progress" has provided the spur to use this power for economic gain. Institutions controlling the ownership and possession of land have, largely, provided the mechanism for such change to occur legitimately.

When change does occur, the effect can be disturbingly dramatic – the felling of a piece of mature woodland; the demolition of a redundant building; the construction of new buildings and roads. The dramatic effect is partly visual, but equally important is the sense of permanence of change – permanence of loss or permanence of addition which, in human terms, may be likened to an amputation or a tattoo – which may require significant adjustment to one's frame of perception before becoming satisfactorily incorporated into it. Invariably these changes refer to property which we do not own ourselves for our own personal enjoyment and benefit, yet we are affected and often feel we have an "interest" in the land whether or not this would be recognised by the law. This introduces notions of collective enjoyment, social responsibility, common property rights, communal rights, etc.

The ethical validity of private property rights, which it might be argued are simply the creation of lawyers, has been challenged and questioned by many philosophers. It must be remembered that "property" is a social institution. If social welfare is better served by shifting land from the private sector to the public sector, the State has the power to effect such a shift. It has the power of eminent domain by which it can compel the release of land in private ownership to public use. The State also has the power to reserve a right to claim, on behalf of society, some part of the value of property rights, normally in the form of taxation. It also has the power to tax any income or wealth generated by individual members of society. Indeed, the impact of taxation may have the effect of achieving a change in the pattern of landownership. The notions of property and value derive from society and depend on its structure.

Ownership

It may . . . be said that in the case of a chattel, ownership will be absolute ownership; it is either owned outright by one person (or several persons jointly or in common with each other) or it is not owned at all. In the case of land, however, the law in theory knows no absolute ownership.

(Megarry and Wade 1984)[1]

All land in Britain is technically owned by the Crown and, thus, held directly or indirectly of the Crown. Thus, the matter of ownership is a question of the terms upon which land is held and the duration of those terms. The first of these questions is determined by the doctrine of *tenure* and the second by the doctrine of *estates*.

---

1 Megarry, RE and Wade, HWR (1984) *The Law of Real Property* Stevens & Sons, London.

The doctrine of *tenure* formed part of the foundation of feudal society. In that social structure many forms of tenure existed, though all traced their existence back to the Crown. The law was greatly simplified by the Law of Property Act 1925, which for all practical purposes reduced numerous feudal tenures to one primary form of tenure, namely the freehold.

However, under the feudal system of tenure, whatever the class of tenure, the land might be held for different periods of time. It might be granted for the life of the tenant or for the life of the tenant and the tenant's descendants or for the duration of the lives of any legal heirs of the tenant whether descendants or not. Each of these interests was called an *estate*.

The largest estate in land, the fee simple, has come more and more to resemble absolute ownership, and its proprietor is commonly called the owner of land. This is because the tenurial relationship is now so slender that in practice it can be ignored.

(Megarry and Wade 1984)

The estate associated with freehold tenure could endure in perpetuity and, although this can never be certain, for practical purposes this is assumed to be so. The only other lawful right to the possession of land, known as a tenancy at will, could be ended at any time at the whim of the freeholder. Leaseholds, or terms of years, were not considered part of the feudal system of tenure. They were personal contracts binding only on the parties and not regarded as "real" property. Eventually, however, the law recognised them as proprietary interests; as estates. Once they became acknowledged as estates they were also acknowledged as a form of tenure.

Thus, the modern concept of landownership in Britain relates essentially to the individual ownership of estates and interests in land; the concept of usufruct (the right to enjoy the use and advantages of another's property short of destruction or waste of its substance) is relatively peripheral within the system of English land law. Concepts of communal ownership which lead to land being considered as public domain are secondary to the interests of individual ownership and possession. There is no "right to roam", for example, recognised by the English system of land law. This is, however, simply the product of one form of cultural evolution. When America was a British colony, the English system of land tenure was applied, as was the French system in Quebec. However, the War of Independence swept away the feudally-based system of tenure imposed by the British. The federal government became the owner of land known as public domain. By article IV, section 3 of the Constitution of the United States of America the federal government reserves to itself the right over public domain to control the selling, grant or other disposal of land. A national policy was introduced of alienating public domain land to private property. Indeed, the disposal of public domain land was seen as a major source of revenue for the US Government. Until 1872 when the Yellowstone National Park marked the first step in the establishment of the US National Park system, many assumed that all public domain land would be converted to private ownership. Thus, the notion of public domain is not synonymous with individual freedom of use or access nor any "right to roam".

The "right to roam" is a central feature of the right to navigation which will be examined later. In other respects, however, it is an alien concept to both English and Scottish land law. The Law of Property Act 1925, section 193, did grant a "right of access for air and exercise" to some areas of land; essentially metropolitan commons and commons wholly or partly situated in what, at the time, were referred to as urban districts. The general rule, however, is that members of the public roaming over land belonging to another, without the express or implied consent of the occupier, are treated as trespassers. The Scottish law actually provides a more practical remedy for trespassers to be removed from the land in question than English law.

Many of the aboriginal peoples of the world do not or have not recognised the concept of individual property rights. Rights to use land and natural resources are based instead on the concept of communal ownership. For example,

Under the Maori system of land tenure, rights of occupation and usufruct were divided among sub groups and individuals, but the right of alienation was reserved to the group. Each hapu (section according to line of descent) of the tribe controlled a defined stretch of tribal territory, which it guarded jealously. Trespassers and poachers were punished severely, and persistent border violations led to fighting even between hapu of the same tribe. Within the hapu, whanau, nuclear families and individuals held rights of occupation and use over specific resources; garden plots, fishing-stands, rat-run sections, trees attractive to birds, clumps of flax and shell-fish beds. These they could bequeath to their children. But they could not hand them over to outsiders – even to a spouse – until the hapu as a whole had discussed and approved the transfer; and they had to surrender their claim to particular pieces (though never without recompense) whenever the hapu (or its chief as trustee) required it for other purposes. Similarly, the hapu could alienate no part of its territory without the consent of the rest of the tribe. To put it another way, the rights of the individuals and lesser groups were always subject to the over-right of the greater group. In a real sense, the land was owned ultimately by the tribe. For this reason, an attack on any part of the tribal territory rallied the whole tribe to its defence.

(Metge 1976)[1]

In general, the common law rights of the freeholder (or Crown where appropriate) extend to the airspace above the land to which the estate relates, to a height necessary for the ordinary use and enjoyment of the land and the structures on it. They also extend to the minerals under that land, with the exception of gold, silver, coal, oil and gas. An owner in possession also has a presumed title to any things fixed to or buried in the land, with the exception of treasure trove. There is no right of ownership over wild animals or "fruits of the earth", although a landowner may kill and take such animals under common law, subject to statutory restrictions (such as the Wildlife and Countryside Act 1981). Once dead, they become the property of the landowner.

An estate owner (landlord or tenant) has no property in water which either percolates through the land or flows through it in a defined channel, but may, under common law, draw off any or all percolating water without regard to his neighbours and abstract from other sources subject to return. Unless for domestic use, rights of abstraction are now only exercisable through a system of statutory licensing under the Water Resources Act 1963. The owner also has the sole right to fish in that water, unless there is a right of several fishery granted to another or local inhabitants have acquired fishing rights.

The common law right of a freeholder or leaseholder to develop property exists subject to the proviso that the rights of others are not infringed. In the past, support for this caveat has relied on common law, either by adjudicating on conflicting property rights or by relying on the law of tort (wrongful acts), which includes, in

1 Metge, J (1976) *The Maoris of New Zealand* Routledge & Kegan Paul, London.

particular, nuisance; negligence; the rule in *Rylands* v *Fletcher*; and trespass. It is now more commonly and effectively controlled by statutory restrictions deriving principally from the law of town and country planning and public health. For example, planning permission must be obtained from the appropriate local planning authority in accordance with the appropriate Town and Country Planning Act. The outcome of any application for planning permission under the present system is subject to an extensive body of development control legislation and guidance, and to the contents of statutory plans which outline the policies for the use and development of land in the local authority area.

Public health legislation provides that the use or state of premises must not extend to any statutory nuisance nor be prejudicial to health. For example, the Environmental Protection Act 1990 prohibits the emission of smoke, fumes, gases, dust, steam or smell which could constitute a nuisance or be prejudicial to health; similarly, the accumulation or deposit of substances, the keeping of animals, the production of noise and any other matter declared by any enactment to be a statutory nuisance. Also in the interests of public health, the disposal of household, industrial and commercial waste on land is covered by licences, without which no land can be used for their disposal. To ensure compliance with these stipulations, local authorities have a duty to inspect premises, supported by a right of entry, which they have reason to believe contravene statutory requirements.

In addition to these basic public controls over the utilisation of land and buildings, additional controls are imposed on the utilisation of property with outstanding landscape, architectural, scientific, historical or cultural value. These values are normally identified by one or more of a variety of statutory designations. For example, National Parks; Areas of Outstanding Natural Beauty; Sites of Special Scientific Interest; Environmentally Sensitive Areas; Heritage Coasts and Special Protection Areas. A further designation, Nature Reserves, either National or Local, can be created either by acquisition or agreement negotiated between the owners or occupiers of the land and the relevant statutory body. Management plans and byelaws can be made to protect the reserve including control of public access and prohibition of actions likely to disturb or damage the scientific interest of the reserve. They seldom, however, interfere with the rights of entry and access of the owners and occupiers.

Riparian rights

In the coastal zone most if not all of these designations are limited by the geographical limitations on the policing powers of the responsible public body, which generally do not extend below low-water mark. Internal waters fall under two categories, tidal and non-tidal watercourses. Case law supports the presumption that ownership, whether leasehold or freehold, of the bed of non-tidal watercourses implies the extension of riparian rights adjacent to the watercourse to the soil of the bed of the river *ad medium filium aquae*, the middle of the stream. This applies even where boundaries are drawn on a map along the river bank, unless, of course, an express exception is made in a deed of conveyance . If riparian rights extend to both sides of the river, then the whole bed of the river is under single ownership, provided that the river is not tidal. While there is a general presumption that the riparian owner has the bed of a non-tidal watercourse, there is also a superseding presumption that the owner of a several fishery owns the soil over which the fishery extends unless there is evidence to the contrary. This reflects the separability of the right to the bed of the stream and that to the bank.

Ownership of the bed of a watercourse confers on the owner the common law right to use the property in any legal manner, subject to the provisos that the interests of other riparian owners along the watercourse should not be interfered with; nor should the public right of navigation be obstructed or otherwise interfered with; nor should the stipulations of statutes be contravened. For example, Bates (1990) suggests that placing blocks on the river bed for fishing purposes would be considered a change of use requiring planning permission under the town and country planning legislation. Case law suggests that rights of ownership might, for example, include the construction on the bed of devices for catching fish, providing that the passage of salmon and of other certain species is not restricted; the cutting of reeds; the laying of moorings; and the extraction of sand and other aggregates, subject to the proviso that the extraction does not affect the flow of the water course or its level. The Sea Fisheries (Shellfish) Act 1967 enables a fishery for shellfish to be established on any part of the shore and bed of the sea, or of any estuary or tidal water. It is an offence, within the area of a shellfish bed or private oyster bed, for any other person to disturb or injure the shellfish or the bed of the fishery (except acts associated with the lawful acts of navigation or anchorage); to dredge for any substance except under lawful authority; to deposit any substance; or to place anything prejudicial or likely to be prejudicial to the shellfish bed except for a lawful purpose of navigation or anchorage.

Within the confines of tidal waters and near-shore waters, sediment mobility can give rise over time to the formation of islands. Islands are defined by vegetation coverage and their being dry at all times of the year except during floods. They do not include sandbanks, which are regarded as portions of the submerged land of the "bed". This holds for both tidal and non-tidal waters. In non-tidal waters this causes the redefinition of the *medium filium* between the island and the opposite riparian proprietor. Sediment mobility can also give rise to changes in the channel of a watercourse with repercussions for the concomitant property rights. If the course of a river is subject to rapid change, ownership remains vested in the previous owner of the land, although this ownership may become subject to the rights of the Crown and public associated with such water courses; if the course reverts so will the rights. Where the change is gradual, property rights follow the movement.

While property rights can extend to the banks and bed of a watercourse, the water flowing through them is not capable of private possession in its natural state. Possession can only pertain to that abstracted and then only for the duration of physical possession. Water is a public good and no person is entitled to deprive occupants downstream of a natural flow of water, unless the source is also contained within the property. It is possible, however, for rights of ownership to be granted to an authority by statute. The flow of water should remain substantially unaltered in its quality. Any degradation of water quality might constitute a common law nuisance. This common law right is today supplemented by various statutory provisions which subject all discharges into rivers, estuaries and the sea to the need to obtain the consent of the water authority and to conditions as to the nature, quality and quantity of those discharges. The owner or occupier of land cannot cause or knowingly permit the pollution of water by liquid or matter or impede the proper flow of water so causing the aggravation of a problem from another source.

Possession

The concepts of ownership and of possession are closely related. As a general rule, "Title to land depended on the better right to possession (seisin) rather than vice versa . . . Titles are not absolute but relative; ownership, as between two rival claimants, is the better right to possession" (Megarry and Wade 1984).[1] A squatter, for example, has a title based on his or her own possession and this title is good against everyone except the true owner. Occupation by a tenant is never adverse to the landlord's title.

The owner of an estate in land may grant to another person the right to possession of the land to which the estate relates for a period of years. This is achieved by means of a contract between the parties. The grant is referred to as a lease or tenancy; the grantor is the landlord and the grantee is the lessee or tenant. The leasehold is, like the freehold, an estate in land. Thus, there may be a freehold estate and one or more leasehold estates in the same piece of land (privity of estate). However, the leasehold estate will always terminate at some future date, at which time all the rights contained in the leasehold will revert to the owner of the freehold at that time. If there were no such reversion, what might appear to be a leasehold would, in fact, amount to a freehold estate.

A *lease* is a letting of lands or tenements by a landlord to a tenant. It is a contract for the exclusive possession of the premises by the tenant for the period of the lease, usually in consideration for the payment of a rent.

As long as the lease lasts and the parties are unchanged the landlord, in right of his (or her) reversion, is entitled to receive the rent reserved by the lease; to levy distress on goods and chattels found on the land so as to compel the payment of rent if it is not paid; to bring an action at law against the tenant if he (or she) breaks the covenants of the lease; to enforce a right of re-entry if the tenant breaks the covenants of the lease and the contract so provides; and to claim possession of the land when the tenancy comes to an end. If the landlord disposes of his (or her) interest during the lease the new landlord would have similar rights. The tenant during the lease is entitled to the exclusive possession and quiet enjoyment of the land belonging to the landlord provided that the tenant pays his (or her) rent and performs the

---

1 Megarry, RE and Wade, HWR (1984) *The Law of Real Property*, Stevens & Sons, London.

tenant's obligations under the lease and, if the tenant rightfully disposes of his (or her) interest to another, the new tenant is similarly entitled.

(Walton and Essayan 1982)[1]

It is possible for a person (or group) to be legally entitled (by contract) to receive a benefit from land which the law defines as an *interest* (as distinct from an estate) in the land. Interests in land include: covenants; licences; mortgages; and incorporeal hereditaments (rent charges; advowsons; tithes; easements; profits à prendre; titles of honour; offices).

A *covenant* is a promise contained in a deed between the parties to the promise. Common examples are found in leases and restrictive covenants created on the sale of an estate.

A *licence* is a permission given by the occupier of land (and/or the owner if the owner has reserved this right) which allows the licensee to do some act which would otherwise be a trespass. In these circumstances, the occupant of the premises is in occupation as holder of a licence, not a lease and a licence is not an estate. A lease gives the right to exclusive possession of the land whereas a licence usually does not. For example, a landowner may provide accommodation for an employee who is required to live in the premises provided for the proper performance of his or her duties. If the premises are occupied as a condition of service and no tenancy exists, then the occupant will be a licensee, not a tenant.

The common law distinction between leases and licences is most important. A licence is a simple contract; it is not considered to be real property and the courts will not protect a licensee's right to possession, although they may attempt to construe a licence as a lease. If, for example, a licence purports to confer exclusive possession or involve the payment of rent for a term, the courts may conclude that the parties intended the transaction to be a lease. Genuine licences also fall outside many of the statutory protections afforded other holders of interests in land. Although the courts are not comfortable with the use of licences in relation to land, preferring leases instead, in the marine environment their use is much more important. Generally there are three types of licence: a bare licence; a contractual licence; and a licence coupled with an

---

1 Walton, R and Essayan, M (1982) *Adkin's Landlord and Tenant* 18th ed, Estates Gazette, London.

interest in property. Of these, the latter is particularly relevant to the exploitation of marine resources. A licence which is ancillary to an interest in property such as a profit à prendre and granted by deed or acquired by prescription is, under common law, irrevocable, assignable and enforceable against successors in title of the grantor and the grantee. The importance of licences varies, quite dramatically, across the coastal zone boundaries.

A *mortgage* is a conveyance of a legal or equitable interest in property, with a provision for redemption, ie that upon repayment of a loan or the performance of some other obligation the conveyance shall become void or the interest shall be reconveyed. It is normally used as a means of raising funds for the purchase of an estate secured on the estate itself. It should be distinguished from the following devices:

• *lien* – the right to retain possession of the property of another until a debt is paid;

• *pledge* – a loan of money secured by the possession of chattels delivered to the lender;

• *charge* – similar to a mortgage but a charge conveys nothing; it is merely a conveyance which gives the chargee certain rights over the property as security for the loan.

Incorporeal hereditaments constitute a further category of property consisting of rights related to land but not physical objects. The principal interests in this category are easements and profits à prendre.

Easements are easier to illustrate than define; they include rights of way, rights of light and rights of water. In some respects they have some similarity to restrictive covenants. The definition is too technical to be appropriate here, but involves dominant tenements, servient tenements, benefit, propinquity. An easement is, however, a right exercisable by a landowner by virtue of his or her ownership of an estate in the appropriate land and should be distinguished from what are termed "natural rights", which are simply rights protected by the law of tort, and "public rights", exercisable by anyone in their capacity as a member of the general public. The public rights which most resemble easements are public rights of way.

The common law does not provide a public right to wander, although in certain circumstances a right to wander can be secured in areas of "open country" by agreement with the landowner under the National Parks and Access to the Countryside Act 1949. This contrasts with the ability of any vessel to wander over the surface of the sea and to dwell upon it. A right of way across land, existing as an easement or a licence is not the same as a public right of way. There are broadly three forms of public right of way or "highway": footpaths, bridleways and carriageways, each conferring differing rights on the public. The public may pass along a footpath on foot only; bridleways on foot or horseback; and carriageways by all reasonable forms of vehicular traffic. It is purely a right to pass and repass for legitimate travel, not a right to be on a highway. Ancillary rights, such as a right to pause and admire the view are defined on the basis of reasonableness. Any acts by the public beyond these rights may constitute trespass.

The public right of navigation extends to tidal waters by virtue of their being considered "arms of the sea". This right is, however, qualified, extending only to those watercourses which are physically navigable by the vessels concerned. The public right of navigation does not automatically extend to non-tidal watercourses, even where the bed of the watercourse is vested in a public authority. Navigation rights are incidental to riparian occupation: *Will's Trustees* v *Cairngorm Canoeing & Sailing School* (1976) SLT 162, at p177. A public right can, however, be acquired on the basis of immemorial user; express grant (subject to the approval of the authority responsible for navigation); or statute in relation to watercourses made navigable by works, for example, the River Trent Act 1695 and the Upper Avon Navigation Act 1972. It should be noted that the incidental rights of navigation do not necessarily extend to alighting on adjoining lands other than foreshore; trespass may be committed unless a right is conveyed by agreement or grant from those holding proprietary rights in that land.

As navigational rights are incidental to proprietary rights, other rights are incidental to those of navigation. A riparian owner who also owns the bed of a watercourse can moor boats against the bank or fix moorings to the bed or license others to do so, being incidental to enjoyment of the property (General Development Order 1988 SI 1988 No 1813). This right may, however, be subject to regulation by navigation or conservancy authorities. Whether this right extends to riparian owners who do not own the bed of the watercourse is less clear. Planning permission would be required for a change of use in this instance, just as it is required for all new moorings in rivers and estuaries and on the foreshore above the low-water mark.

Broadly speaking, a *profit à prendre* is a right to take the natural produce from another person's land; for example, it can be a right to take fish, wild game or "fruits of the earth". In terms of ownership, it can be several (exclusive to one person) or in common and either "appurtenant" (attached to and defined by the needs of dominant land) or "in gross" (owned independently of land). A profit in common, which might include rights of common grazing; rights of turbary (cutting turf for fuel); rights of pannage (grazing pigs); rights of estover (timber for repairs to buildings), must be registered on the register of commons to avoid cessation. Certain interests in land are further qualified by customary rights afforded to local inhabitants. Such rights must, however, be ancient, continuous, certain and reasonable. They include such as the right of fishermen of a particular parish to dry their nets on private land: *Mercer* v *Denne* (1905) 2 Ch 538, CA.

Proof of title

It is clear that the "bundle of rights" associated with the ownership and possession (rights to use or not use) of land are more abstruse than mere common sense might suggest. Explaining the existence of these rights is one thing, but how is one to know that they exist; how is one to know the extent to which a "full set" of rights has been disaggregated and the extent of the practical ramifications of any such disaggregation? To some extent it depends upon who is asking the question, but more particularly how property rights are recorded (in both form and content); how complete the record; and how accessible the information.

Proof of a right to use and possession depends on the ability to provide proof of good title. Although most rights to use or occupy land are granted by contractual agreement, more particularly, such agreements are invariably required to be in the form of a deed. Deeds are written documents which have been properly witnessed and verified. Possession of the deeds becomes crucially important in demonstrating the existence of good title. Even so, tracing the existence of all deeds and public rights can be rather hit and miss. To overcome the deficiencies of relying solely on the evidence of deeds, the government has, for many years, been slowly introducing a system of compulsory registration of title. Since 1925 there has been a succession of Land Registration Acts. The Land

Registry is now charged with examining the title to particular land; preparing an authoritative record of title, describing it with the rights it enjoys, identifying the present owner and disclosing rights of third parties and encumbrances to which the land is subject. The State guarantees that the title will not be disturbed as long as the present owner (registered proprietor) remains in possession or in receipt of rent and profits from the land (Ruoff and Pryer 1990)[1]. To all intents and purposes entry on the Land Registry is proof of good title.

Transferability

In a mercantile as distinct from feudal economy, different notions of value dictated that although valuable assets must be secure (in the sense of safe from theft) they must also be capable of being traded. Property must, therefore, be transferable and "portable". The notion of trading land is relatively recent and only became commonplace during the 19th century. One of the first popular illustrations of this trend is found in *Great Expectations* written by Charles Dickens in 1860.

The feudal system of tenure did not provide real property with "portability". However, the feudal services upon which feudal tenure was based proved to be adaptable to a mercantile equivalent. The emphasis on property rights, rather than land itself, ostensibly gave land a degree of "portability" which otherwise it so conspicuously lacked because "rights" are capable of being divided, shared and transferred in a manner which is impossible for land itself. The provision of feudal service in return for the possession of land gradually became commuted into money equivalents. Property rights became capable of translation into rights to receive cash payments, often on a regular basis as an income flow. The right to receive such cash flows, in effect, became as "portable" as personal property, particularly negotiable instruments.

Nevertheless, the transfer of a legal estate can be fraught with difficulty. Transfers tend, therefore, to be slow by comparison with the transfer of personal property; they normally require skilled professional advice; they tend to be expensive and, in addition, a target for taxation. Although, in some respects it would be

---

1 Ruoff, TBF and Pryer, EJ (1990) *Land Registration Handbook* Sweet & Maxwell, London.

convenient if transfers of property rights could be undertaken informally. To do so, however, would put at risk the substantial protection which the law bestows on real property. For this reason transactions involving the transfer of property rights continue to be both expensive and slow.

Freeholders have always shown an understandable reluctance to part with the closest thing to absolute ownership of land unless absolutely necessary. A lease enables them to part with immediate possession and quiet enjoyment of the property while retaining the right to the reversion of possession to the freeholder. Leases can be quicker and cheaper to transfer than the freehold. It is a conveyance by which the landlord transfers a portion of his or her interest in the land to a tenant for a period of years. A lease is never a conveyance of the entire interest which a landlord possesses in the land; such a conveyance, if made by deed, would be an assignment and not a lease. Only a "term" is granted to the tenant, the landlord always retaining a reversion.

The coastal zone

The framework of property rights is relatively well developed for land-based resources yet tends to remain ill-defined and ambiguous in inaccessible areas, notably in the marine environment where the concept of individual ownership of property rights is less powerful than that of common property rights. Quite dramatic variations in the nature of property rights occur across the land–sea interface and become critically important in considering the planning and management of the coastal zone.

The coastal zone is essentially a narrow band of land and sea around the coastline. In the USA it is defined as "the coastal waters . . . and the adjacent shorelands . . . strongly influenced by each other, and in proximity to the shorelines" (Coastal Zone Management Act 1972, 16 United States Code Annotated 1453). It is an area in which the natural environment and human activity not only interact with each other, but also traverse the land-sea divide. In the UK the nature of coastal zone property rights is contingent on the divisions in English law associated with the coastal zone. There is no legal recognition of the concept of a unified coastal zone; several different classifications apply to coastal land and water, most notably: *terra firma*, foreshore, seabed and internal waters.

According to English common law, the foreshore lies between high-water mark and low-water mark with *terra firma* (dry land) above it and seabed below. The high-water mark boundary is more precisely defined as the line of ordinary high tides, that is the "line of the medium high tide between the springs and neaps ascertained by taking the average of these medium tides during the year": *Tracey Elliott* v *Earl of Morley* (1907) 51 SJ 625. The low-water mark boundary is defined in a corresponding manner. In Scotland a more expansive definition of foreshore is applied, extending down to ordinary spring tides or those of greatest range following each full and new moon. Internal waters (estuaries, rivers and bays) occur on the land side of the territorial sea baseline. The baseline is, in general, taken to be the low-water line around the coast as marked on Admiralty charts. Bays are delineated through the identification of points on the coast where the indentation begins and a line of not more than 24 miles in length stretching across the mouth of the bay.

Maps and charts are the primary source of information for ascertaining boundaries for modern conveyancing purposes. Maps based on Ordnance Survey data utilise the legal definition of high- and low-water marks. Admiralty charts, however, rely on different reference points. The variation in projection, age and terminology of these sources can cause significant confusion over boundary delimitation between *terra firma*, the foreshore, the seabed and internal waters.

The legal definition of foreshore does not necessarily correspond to the natural feature since the 17th-century treatise De Jure Maris eliminated equinoctial and spring tides from the foreshore definition. Furthermore, areas of gently sloping beach can potentially be excluded from the English definition of foreshore. The natural processes of accretion and encroachment also result in a temporal variation to the legal definition of foreshore. The property rights associated with the foreshore track the line of the tides as long as the changes are slow, gradual and imperceptible. Determination of whether a change is slow, gradual and imperceptible may not be clear cut. For example, the influence of the tide can be difficult to ascertain in estuaries where the water level is affected by the flow of a river as well as by the tide. This source of ambiguity has given rise to a distinction between tidal and non-tidal streams, tidal waters being defined as territorial waters in which there is a perceptible lateral ebb and flow in the ordinary and regular course of events.

In the present context, some of the most notable features of the English law of real property which differ between *terra firma*, the foreshore and seabed include:

- the definition of property rights by precise association with clearly delineated territorial boundaries;
- protection of the right to possession for the lawful owners of an estate or interest in land;
- the dominant power of freehold ownership;
- the ability to transfer property rights from one owner to another;
- reluctance to protect public access to "common goods" without specific authority;
- control of un-neighbourly use of land by financial penalty under the law of tort, often reinforced by statute;
- protection of the rights of licensees or members of the public by financial sanctions but not possession.

Tidal watercourses

A tidal river or creek extends from the highest point inland where the tides regularly ebb and flow to the point where it enters the sea. English common law has long regarded tidal watercourses as arms of the sea and, consequently, subject to the special rules concerning the ownership of the seabed and foreshore. It should be noted, however, that there could be a disparity between the common law interpretation of the seaward extent of tidal waters (ie the general line of the coast at low-water mark) and that adopted for international legal purposes, namely a straight line across the mouth of the river between points on the low-tide line of its banks.

The beds of all tidal watercourses and estuaries or arms of the sea which are generally navigable are *prima facie* vested in the Crown. This property is subject to the public rights of navigation and fishery, where no private right of fishery exists. Because this ownership is independent of the adjoining lands, the presumption that riparian owners are also owners of the bed *ad medium filium* does not apply in tidal waters. In certain instances Crown ownership of the bed of tidal waters has become vested in a harbour or other statutory authority in accordance with the Harbours Act 1964. Moreover, examples of private ownership of the bed of tidal rivers do exist, for example, the Beaulieu River in Hampshire, deriving from a royal grant in the 13th century.

Foreshore

At common law, the foreshore is *prima facie* assumed to be vested in the Crown unless good title can be proved by actual or presumed existence of a grant or prescription by the Crown. There has been relatively little challenge to the Crown's claim to ownership of the foreshore. The Crown Lands Act 1829 transferred the Crown's interest in the foreshore, along with its land revenues and responsibilities for management and improvement, to the Commissioners of Woods, now the Crown Estates Commissioners. They currently retain responsibility for about half of the foreshore of the United Kingdom. The Crown Estates Act 1961, amended by the Miscellaneous Financial Provisions Act 1983, enables the Commissioners to grant leases for periods of up to 150 years or issue licences (for minor works and dredging) on parcels of land selected at their discretion. This power is subject to the caveat that they must obtain the best consideration in money or money's worth which, in their opinion, can reasonably be obtained. They may impose any covenants, conditions or restrictions they think fit, which can be enforced by a right of re-entry under the Crown Estate Act 1961.

Private holdings include: the foreshores in Cornwall; certain areas in the County of Durham leased by the Bishop of Durham prior to 1858 and now vested in the Church Commissioners; and other landholdings around the coastline of England and Wales. Private rights of ownership over the foreshore are subject to certain conditions and other interests, such as: the rights and duties of the coast protection authorities; byelaws made under the Military Lands Act 1900 (applying to firing ranges and sea adjacent to Ministry of Defence property); the public rights of fishery and navigation; rights of several (private) fishery; and the law of public nuisance.

Defence of the realm is an historic duty, of imperfect obligation, owed by the Crown under common law which is not transferred or diminished with the transfer of proprietary rights. This includes defence of the realm from the sea. The Coast Protection Act 1949 charges coast protection authorities with separate coastal protection duties. They have the power to purchase land, either compulsorily or by agreement, for the construction of works in relation to this duty. Their consent is also required for any other person to carry out coast protection work (other than work of maintenance or repair).

Proprietary rights are more generally subject to the public rights of fishery and navigation where the foreshore is covered by tidal water. As a right of ancient times, the right to fish has fallen under the protection of the Crown as *parens patriae*. The rights of the Crown and of any person holding a grant in the soil of the foreshore are subject to the right of owners of adjoining land to have access to the sea at all times for purposes of the public right of navigation. This does not necessarily imply, however, universal existence of ancillary rights, for example, a public right to cross the foreshore to fish or navigate in the sea or in tidal waters.

Where a statute, agreement or access order permits public access to privately owned foreshore, the owner of the land may not do anything on the foreshore which would substantially reduce the public right of access. This right can, however, be restricted where the ownership of the foreshore lies with the Crown. The Crown Estates Commissioners have powers under the Crown Estate Act 1961 to make regulations regarding use of the foreshore, even to the point of restricting the common law rights of navigation and fishery. The Public Health Act 1936 as amended by the Local Government (Miscellaneous Provisions) Act 1976 grants local authorities the power to make byelaws in respect of public bathing and pleasure boating on or from the foreshore.

Right to bathe

A right of access to the foreshore does not necessarily extend to a right to bathe or the pursuit of recreation (including wildfowling) on the foreshore. While the Crown or grantees of the foreshore hold that land for the benefit of the public, recreational activities are not considered to fall under this definition. However, many activities have been generally tolerated on the foreshore without giving rise to any legal right to continue them. The policy of the courts, however, in respect of bathing from Crown foreshore, has been to avoid enforcing any unnecessary or injurious restraint where no mischief or injury is likely to arise. A right to bathe (and ancillary access) may be acquired by agreement under the National Parks and Access to the Countryside Act 1949, as amended by the Local Government Act 1974. It may also be acquired by prescription or statute, for the benefit of the public in general or the inhabitants of a particular district.

Right of fishery

In exceptional circumstances, a private right to fish may exist, for example, in cases where the grant of a private right to fish by the Crown was established as having existed prior to the Magna Carta. Generally, however, private rights are now dependent on statutory authority. The right to fish does not extend to the collection of seaweed, nor does it allow for the use of all fishing gears; it does, however, extend to the taking of shellfish. It is accompanied by incidental rights of temporary anchoring and temporary mooring (provided that the exercise of these rights does not cause an obstruction to navigation), beaching and grounding, for which the riparian owner can extract no charge unless additional benefits are provided or it occurs within a harbour. Exercising a right to fish requires access to water. This may be limited to places which, through necessity or usage, are statutorily appropriated for the purpose or where the right is acquired by custom. The right to fish cannot be assumed to include any rights over the soil of the foreshore and must not interfere with the right of navigation. It should be noted, furthermore, that there are numerous statutory qualifications to the public right of fishery.

Seabed

As a general rule, a right of passage over the sea exists at common law for ships, boats and other vessels for the purposes of navigation, commerce, trade and intercourse. The public right of navigation is a "right to wander" which supersedes the property rights of the Crown and their grantees: *Gann* v *Free Fishers of Whitstable* (1865) 11 HL Cas 192. However, the seabed beneath British territorial waters is claimed as the property of the Crown, although the Crown's right has not been judicially decided. The Crown's claim to the seabed was first proposed by Thomas Digges in the 16th century and has never seriously been challenged since. Although the present balance of argument supporting the Crown's claim to proprietary rights over the seabed derives from the Scottish courts, its applicability to English law is generally accepted.

Historical debate concerning the extent of the proprietary rights of the Crown in and over the seabed has been hampered by historic inability to perceive the seabed as being of active use or value. The Crown Estate Act 1961 limits the right of the Crown to surrender ownership to charitable and public purposes. As with the foreshore, leases of up to 150 years and licences typify the means by which the Crown's interest in the seabed is transferred to its subjects. Private ownership in the seabed is rare; indeed, no consideration is given to private ownership of the seabed in contemporary legislation, for example, the Protection of Wrecks Act 1975. This results partly from the Crown Estate Act 1961, but also the Crown Lands Act 1702 which forbade the alienation of Crown lands in England and Wales. Gibson (1978)[1] suggests that the net effect of the two Acts means that any claim for private ownership has to prove a root of title originating before the reign of Queen Anne if it were to be successful.

As consequence of the Crown's ownership of the seabed, the Crown has rights of alienation in respect of its interests in the resources of the seabed and its substrata. These are generally exercised by the grant of licences. In practical terms there is little difference between leases and licences with regard to utilisation of the seabed. The characteristics adopted by the courts to distinguish between leases and licences on land have little meaning in a marine environment. The practical difficulty in ensuring that a lessee may rely on "quiet enjoyment of the property" may be insurmountable. As a result, licences are of greater interest for the exploitation of the resources of the seabed. Nevertheless, the forms adopted by Crown for leases for the foreshore and seabed are relatively standard. Contractual licenses apply to prospecting, dredging operations and hydrocarbon exploitation.

Further restrictions on the exercise of property rights are generally based on the grounds of safety, for example, restrictions imposed on activities in the general position of submarine cables and pipelines under the Submarine Telegraph Act 1885. The powers of local authorities under the Public Health Act 1961 to make byelaws restricting property rights through the regulation of recreational activities out to 1,000m seawards of the low-water mark also fall into this category, as do the powers of the Minister of Defence to provide for public safety in military exercise areas.

In accordance with the Petroleum (Production) Act 1934, licences

---

1 Gibson, J (1978) The ownership of the seabed under British territorial waters, *International Relations* 6.

in respect of hydrocarbon extraction, like those for the extraction of aggregates below high-water mark, are of the nature of a concession by the Crown of some of its rights to a private party under a commercial transaction. Licences relating to the extraction of hydrocarbons, reflecting the formal rules prescribed by Parliament for their issue, form and content, have a strong regulatory flavour. They are based on model clauses derived from the Petroleum (Production) Regulations. A licence to search for and get petroleum bestows exclusivity of possession for the specified duration of the licence. It conveys no right of ownership of hydrocarbons in situ, but it does entitle the licensee to ownership of all petroleum which the licensee may extract under licence. There is some debate, therefore, as to whether a petroleum licence constitutes a proprietary interest of profit à prendre which the courts would protect against any act or behaviour which diminishes the value of the licensee's interest. Nevertheless, a petroleum licence is acknowledged as a vested right entitled to protection under international law.

Normally, the exercise of rights conveyed on the seabed, as with the foreshore, is subject to qualifications or restrictions, such as the public rights of fishery and navigation. Contrary to the complex picture above low-water mark, there is only one conservation designation (Marine Nature Reserves) which presently affects property rights below low-water mark. These are defined under section 36 of the Wildlife and Countryside Act 1981 as areas designated within an area of

land covered (continuously or intermittently) by tidal waters or parts of the sea in or adjacent to Great Britain up to the seaward limits of territorial waters for their nature conservation interest.

While there are byelaw-making powers relating to Marine Nature Reserves, only two reserves have yet been designated. Furthermore, the byelaws cannot interfere with the rights and functions of any person and authority, including private rights and public rights of fishery and navigation.

Conclusions

The division of the coastal zone into four categories in terms of property rights presents the practitioner with a complex scene of ambiguity and uncertainty. The boundaries between these categories can be imprecise. The derivation of marine property rights from inappropriate extension of concepts developed for terrestrial applications is not well suited to the use and development of marine resources. While the rationalisation of coastal zone property rights could be proposed as a solution to the problem of complexity and ambiguity, realistically, the practitioner has no option but to come to terms with the numerous elements discussed in the preceding discussion.

Further reading

Alder, J (1989) *Development Control* 2nd ed, Sweet & Maxwell, London.

Bettelheim, B (1986) *The Informed Heart* Penguin, London.

Chappelle, D (1992) *Land Law*, Pitman, London.

Gadsden, GD (1988) *The Law of Commons* Sweet & Maxwell, London.

Gordon, WM (1989) *Scottish Land Law* W Green & Son, Edinburgh.

Lawson, FH and Rudden, B (1982) *The Law of Property* 2nd ed, Clarendon Press, Oxford.

McAuslan, P (1975) *Land, Law and Planning* Weidenfeld & Nicolson, London.

Reader, J (1988) *Man on Earth* William Collins Sons & Co, London.

For a more detailed account of property rights in the coastal zone, see: Seabrooke, W and Pickering, H (1994) "The Extension of Property Rights to the Coastal Zone", *Journal of Environmental Management* 42: 161–179.

CHAPTER 2

Trusts

Synopsis
Strict settlement – Its original purposes – Its unpopularity with
tenant-for-life and Exchequer – Tax penalties – Gradual demise.
Other trusts meeting same and new objectives – Charitable Land
Trusts – Essentially a disposal of landowner's interest – Formed to
meet charitable purposes – May include preservation of estate –
Taxation of such trusts.

Strict settlement

Trusts have a long history in English chancery law, the most
important of which, the strict settlement, grew to contain three
elements which are to be found in most trusts involving the landed
estate.

1 Entail or conditional gift

First, the *entail* or *conditional gift*. The practice of granting land to
a man and his heirs male, thus restricting succession, met a natural
wish of a family to preserve their inheritance. In the early days in the
12th and 13th centuries it did more than that. At a time when land
was one of the few forms of wealth and money as such was in short
supply, it met the need to find some means of recompense which
would tie a retainer to the land and ensure that he could meet the
feudal requirements of his king – namely that he could appear in the
feudal host with the requisite number of men-at-arms. With land the
lord could offer houses and means of livelihood to these retainers
without whom his feudal role was lost. It was natural that he should
wish to preserve intact the estate for his heirs so that their feudal
status could also be maintained. In the Magna Carta of 1217 the
right of alienation was limited by the provision that the tenant-in
chief must not give or sell to anyone so much of his estate as to

make it incapable of furnishing the due service to his lord[1]. Gifts of land which precluded alienation by the heir, the forerunner of family settlements, were protected by De Donis Conditionabilis (concerning conditional gifts) 1285 in the reign of Edward I.

2 Life interest

The statute of Mortmain of 1279, forbidding gifts of land to corporations, established a second principle of the settlement of land. In this case the statute was motivated by a desire to avoid land being locked away in perpetuity so that the Crown lost the recurring opportunity to extract a tax imposed on an heir succeeding to his father's estates. The courts have always opposed the efforts of landowners and their lawyers to establish permanent settlements. In line with Magna Carta, legislation was enacted – the Statute of Uses 1285, protecting the entail. However, by a legal device, the "common recovery", the current tenant of the estate was enabled to break the entail by a legal fiction. He reverted to the position of freeholder in absolute possession and the entail was broken. Suffice it to say, lawyers, to counter this, sought more permanent settlements and the Statute of Uses 1535, while recovering for the Crown some of the fiscal rights denied it by a successful entail, confirmed the tenant-for-life (as he became known) in the possession of the legal estate. This feature, the *life interest*, was and remains the second element of the strict settlement. The tenant-for-life had a legal estate in the property, but only for his life and not absolutely. However, so long as there were no heirs, there were no ultimate beneficiaries to protect the estate from depredation, giving the life tenant a free rein to destroy or "waste" the properties. Nor could equity in the person of the Lord Chancellor intervene in the absence of beneficiaries to seek his aid.

3 Appointment of trustees

The third feature of the strict settlement was in effect a solution to this problem. It provided for the *appointment of trustees*, whose legal duty was to protect the estate for those to whom it was entailed. Over the years the extent of the settlement was limited in accordance with principles of law that came to govern all settlements and in the 18th century the length of a settlement was

---

1 Magna Carta 1217 art 39.

limited to life or lives in being plus 21 years.

4 Social effects of strict settlement

The effects of the strict settlement had a profound effect on the social history of this country. Through historical necessity settlements tended to primogeniture, usually through the male line. This in turn ensured that estates were kept intact in the hands of the eldest son, while younger children were forced to go out and seek other means of livelihood even if they were provided with a limited income from their eldest brother's estate known as "portions". The safeguarding of the settlement allowed women to succeed as tenants-for-life and protected their inheritance from their husband's greed or need, as the case might be.

Although in law every settlement would come to an end when the last person named in the entail as tenant-for-life came of age, in practice the recurring need of each generation for money ensured its perpetuation if the trustees so wished. An opportunity arose for the last named in the entail to break the entail before his death with the permission of the trustees, who would then advance him that ready cash on condition he was made a life tenant once again but naming his son as future life tenant and the son's son a tenant in tail.

The settlement also protected landowners from the avarice of the Crown or the results of backing the wrong side in a civil war or the penalties of recusancy should they espouse the wrong religion. It is tempting to suggest that John Hampden's refusal to pay ship-money was engineered by those opposed to autocratic government who chose a tenant-for-life knowing his estates could not be forfeited for his actions.

The extraordinary way in which landed estates remained in the family, often unimpaired, surely owed much to the strict settlement. It can be no accident that of the five members impeached by Charles I but subsequently acquitted, the families of Pym, Hampden and Hazelrigg, or their lineal successors, still to this day occupy estates they held in the 17th century. Among other parliamentarians, Fiennes (Lord Saye and Sele), Verney and Eliot remain owning their family estates to this day.

In the same context it is equally interesting to note, when looking at sale particulars of estates sold as late as the 1940s and 1950s, that so often they comprise whole parishes where the minimum of alienation has occurred. A further result of the settlement inhibiting the sale of settled property until at least 1882 was that the landlord and tenant system survived so that even at the turn of the 19th century almost 90% of the land was tenanted.

5 Demise of the strict settlement

The freedom for the tenant-for-life to sell property after the Settled Land Act of 1882, even if the capital money was protected, combined with the fiscal attack through estate duty introduced in 1894 by Lord Harcourt, weakened the territorial integrity of the landed estate. Even the concessionary rates provided in the Finance Act 1925 and prevailing in 1949, which maintained the 1919 rates of duty on *agricultural* property, imposed a top rate of tax of 30% on estates over £1m and 40% over £2m. Other non-agricultural property came to be taxed at progressively higher rates.

Although there are still estates held under strict settlements as the entail works its way through, such family arrangements are no longer encouraged by professional advisers. One reason may be that as estates grow smaller through sales to raise death duties, there is a real need to retain flexibility for the family to raise cash for capital expenses and emergencies. Even school fees in a medium-sized family may be outside the reach of income after tax. Then again the increasing trend to equalise each child's share in a will militates against the principle of the settlement as a means of keeping the inheritance intact. It is, however, the adverse tax treatment of strict settlements which has finally reduced them to history. A system whereby each successive tenant-for-life took a legal estate and paid estate duty was in direct contrast to other forms of trusts with an interest in possession where duty was paid on the death of the donor and beneficiaries escaped further duty as they became entitled to the estate.

Other trusts

Of more recent history other forms of trust have become more extensively used to meet those needs served by the strict settlement after the latter had become too vulnerable to capital taxation. Of prime importance remained the desire of the donor to ensure that a bequest be passed on to succeeding members of the family with whom it had been historically associated. Conversely, a trust might be used to spread the income or benefit of an estate around members of a family and not to the heir only. Where such a bequest was made when beneficiaries were still young and their needs and abilities were still unknown, the problem of who was to be given what could be met by a discretionary trust leaving the trustees to make decisions as to apportioning income and capital over the years.

A trust can be used to protect a wife's property and this was of considerable importance prior to the Married Women's Property Act 1883. Conversely, as the courts have increasingly awarded divorced wives considerable sums of money from the husband's estate or future income, so families have tried to protect the husband's property accordingly. The cost of this to the beneficiary is that he has no legal estate in the property and, unlike the tenant-for-life, no positive power over the acquisition and disposal of capital assets.

Tax avoidance

Of overriding importance, certainly since the turn of the century, has been the need for families to protect their property from the incidence of estate duty. The strict settlement was shown to be vulnerable since the tenant-for-life was regarded as the legal owner and, on his death, duty was payable to the value of the estate as it passed down to the appointed heir. For a time, after the Second World War, tax advisers used the device of a discretionary trust, which vested the legal estate in the trustees and, unless they so determined, did not vest the legal estate in any beneficiary. While the law against perpetuities brought this state of affairs to an end at the latest on the coming of age of the unborn child, it ensured that for two generations the estate escaped death duties. However, capital transfer tax, introduced in 1975, imposed a tax levied every 10 years at one-third of the lifetime rate of duty on a discretionary trust. As the rates of tax then were relatively high, most trustees of discretionary trusts took advantage of the option then given to them to terminate the trust and apportion the estate to the beneficiary or to a trust with an interest in possession, which effectively meant that a member of the family acquired a legal estate in the property and duty would be payable on his death. It is interesting to see how the Crown has found it fiscally desirable to ensure that inheritance occurs, thus providing an opportunity to tax it.

For some years, until 1985, the skilful use of the trust in other forms which attracted minimum duty, mitigated the effects of capital transfer tax. With the introduction of inheritance tax, of the potentially exempt transfer and more recently of 100% relief for business assets and some farmland, the threat to the family estate from capital taxation has largely disappeared. Inheritance tax became, with good fortune, a largely avoidable tax and in theory family dispositions of property could be made on other than fiscal grounds. Nevertheless, few owners or their advisers can shut their eyes to the fact that the distribution of wealth by means of taxation remains on the political agenda and families will continue to pass on their estates often before it is really advisable for them to do so, to avoid the effects of a revision of legislation.

The charitable land trust

A charitable land trust is essentially not a tax saving device for an individual, though it may deny taxes to the State. When land is put into such a trust, the settlor (in this context the former landowner) forgoes not just the payment of income tax, capital gains tax and taxes on assets transferred, he forgoes all income and all capital from the lands in the trust; he also, of course, forgoes expenditure. In exchange he gains the assurance that the subject-matter of the trust will be maintained and managed for the future within the boundaries and for the purposes laid down in the trust deed of which he will have been the chief author.

Objectives

A charitable land trust may be formed with the prime object of preserving a sector of land and buildings for the benefit of the community in general and for those who live on the land concerned; but in law and for the trust to be acceptable to the Charity Commissioners and the Inland Revenue, the charitable purposes of the trust must fall within one or more of four categories, namely:

(a) for the relief of poverty;
(b) for the advancement of education;
(c) for the advancement of religion;
(d) for other purposes beneficial to the community.

The objectives of the average charitable trust will almost certainly fall into the fourth category, though it may also encompass one or more of the other three. The fourth category would include such purposes as: the protection of the countryside; the conservation of a particular garden or building of special merit; the conservation of wildlife; the preservation of the environment; and the promotion of agriculture. The preservation of an estate "as a unit" is unlikely to be accepted as a charitable purpose unless it can be linked to public benefit or to one of the other categories. It should be appreciated, however, that for the trust to be "beneficial to the community" its purposes must be widely enough drawn to include a reasonably large section of the community and not be confined to the benefit of particular individuals.

There is a difference, of course, between the land itself being the charitable object of the trust and the land being one of the assets of the trust through the use of which the charitable purposes are carried out. Where the land (or of course a building of particular merit) is the object of the trust then it will, normally, be necessary that it be open to the public for a minimum period in the year, currently in the region of 90 days; where, on the other hand, the land is merely an asset of the trust, public access, other things being equal, will be immaterial, the land being used to provide income to be used for its own upkeep and to be applied for the charitable purposes of the trust. Land, as an asset of the trust, may be bought and sold, but the use of the proceeds of any sale will be restricted.

If the settlor or his family wish to remain in occupation of, say the principal house on an estate owned by a charitable land trust (for whatever charitable purpose), they must not derive any personal benefits from such occupation (other than those which are merely incidental to their occupation) and the trust property which they occupy must be let to them at a full rent and generally on terms which would be applied to any lessee.

Although in most cases the freehold of land is transferred to a charity it is possible in "appropriate cases" to grant a long lease to a charity. The terms of the proposed lease will be carefully scrutinised by the Charity Commission and the length of it will have to be appropriate to the property transferred and to the charitable purposes of the trust.

Trading venture and taxation

Since the Charity Commissioners will have to accept the charity as
an appropriate one, operating under a deed properly drawn up and
administered, it is only prudent in practice to consult them from the
outset and to follow an established precedent if possible. It must
not be forgotten that the Inland Revenue is given an opportunity to
object to a proposed charity being registered and although the
Charity Commissioners are the body which gives final approval,
they will not do so in the face of substantial Inland Revenue
objection.

Since the laws of taxation are subject to fairly frequent change it
is not appropriate in the present context to explore the current
taxation, or non-taxation, of charitable trusts, but it is worth
mentioning the position of any trading venture undertaken by a
charity. The profits arising from a trade carried on by a charity are
exempt from income tax only if they are applied solely for the
purposes of the charity and the trade is either carried on as part of
the main purpose of the charity or carried out primarily by the
beneficiaries of the charity. These are conditions not necessarily
easily fulfilled so that in the majority of cases the trading activities
of a charity will be subject to tax. The problem is often avoided by
the establishment of a separate company to undertake the trading,
which then covenants the profits to the charity as charges on
income, pays them under deduction of tax and the charity reclaims
the tax from the Inland Revenue. In order for the relief not to be lost;
the payments under covenant must be made within the tax year.
This can be difficult, for the company's profits may well not be
known in time to do this. In practice the normal arrangement is to
covenant a fixed sum (in line with expected profits) which can be
paid within the tax year concerned, the charity repaying the
difference between the fixed sum and the company's profits if the
former turns out to be too high. It is advisable that these
arrangements be known to the Revenue in advance.

CHAPTER 3

The place of territory

Synopsis
Needs of man: identity, stimulation, security – Defence of territory –
Distinction between ownership and occupation – Good management
– Element of choice.

Introduction

A book on aspects of landownership must mention the landowner,
but it is not possible to write of such a person as an individual for
each is different and while the problems which landowners have to
face in the use and management of their estates are similar, every
owner's approach to them is not. There will be differences in
understanding, in attitude and in the acceptance or rejection of
responsibilities: furthermore, of course, problems and
responsibilities differ with the extent and make-up of estates. An
owner-occupier of an 800-ha arable farm in East Anglia will face
problems and demands very different in type and extent from those
arising on a similar sized estate made up of small rented farms in
the West Country. It is only possible, therefore, to deal with
landownership in the general, rather than in the specific, sense,
ranging perhaps from that of a house and some land in the country
to that of a large country estate or to a landowning institution.

Needs

Robert Ardrey in his book *The Territorial Imperative* says, "A man's
devotion to his territory is deeper than his devotion to the woman
who shares his bed"[1]. Furthermore, he points out that man as a
species has three needs to sustain a worthwhile life, namely identity
(the opposite of which is anonymity), stimulation (the opposite of

---

1 Ardrey, R (1967) *The Territorial Imperative* Harper Collins, London.

which is boredom) and security (the opposite of which is anxiety). The holding of territory – and the reader may interpret this word in any appropriate way – can satisfy these needs. As an owner of land a person has an identity – and the degree of ownership by and large does not matter so long as it is sustainable over an acceptable period. An individual who has no house, who lives in a cardboard box on the Embankment or who has to sleep rough in the doorway of a shop, has no identity within the community. Such individuals may be a cause for concern, often thought of as someone else's responsibility. They can be ignored. With no fixed address an individual hardly exists.

The owner of land has an opportunity to use and enjoy it. He has, further, an opportunity, or perhaps a necessity, to protect it. He can remain busy and vigilant. He can tend his garden. He can say "Trespassers will be prosecuted". He may be able to farm the land and in the process to think and plan. He can allow another to use it while himself remaining concerned with how that use is exercised. He can, then, use and manage the land, watch over it and "fight" for it. As a landowner he need never be bored.

The owner of land is socially and legally sheltered within the community and materially assured by his right to occupy and own. A man owning nothing is essentially anonymous, bored and anxious. The defence of territory (and "defence" in the modern world does not necessarily imply confrontation) provides identity and stimulation. The holding of territory provides security.

Defence of territory

The need to occupy and defend territory is an animal instinct common to most species, while the need to acquire and own land without occupying it is not. Nomadic tribes do not, in Western understanding, "own" land; they occupy it and move on. They may, in their understanding, own rights of occupation and use over the whole area across which they habitually roam. Where, in this sense, does ownership begin? What rights were the settlers in the New World usurping when they occupied the lands over which Indian tribes habitually hunted and wandered? When does occupation fade into ownership – whether ownership be for a term of years or in perpetuity? Does it depend on land use, the need to settle and "farm"? If ownership is theft, as some still like to affirm, from whom in the first place did the theft take place and who was the original thief? Ownership without occupation is essentially a phenomenon of "civilisation". In primitive communities, as in the animal world, occupation is synonymous with ownership so that without occupation there can be no ownership; to most societies, however, ownership (though only really a legal fiction) is distinct from occupation and each may be held in different hands without impinging on the other. Occupation is one thing, a part, though not the whole, of ownership. Thus, the occupier who is not the owner holds a lesser right than the owner and the owner who has parted with occupation holds a lesser right than he did. Devotion to defensible space stems from occupation. The occupier will defend his territory even though he does not fully own it and the owner will defend his territory even though he does not fully occupy it.

Man is a clubbable animal and defends and enjoys his own where "his own" is something with which he can feel associated and on which he is able to exercise some degree of influence. Thus, most responsible people will care for their own homes even if their ownership is limited in degree. Furthermore, if their senses of belonging and of responsibility extend beyond the confines of their immediate home, they are often willing to co-operate with others to care for and defend a wider space. A village can be such a space as can a larger area seen as a unit like an estate in recognisable ownership. Recognition in this form, however, only arises from one of two sources, either from a cohesive sense of community brought about by enlightened and sympathetic management of the whole which everyone can recognise, or from a sense of antagonism which encourages co-operation between the oppressed (the outcome of bad management?).

The landowner who has voluntarily parted with certain rights of occupation (eg by letting for a defined period) has in the process retained others. First, he has retained the right to resume full occupation at the conclusion of the lease, however far in the future that may be; he has also reserved certain rights to reoccupy where the tenant defaults, together with other rights and obligations connected with the property. He will require the lessee to undertake specified acts of maintenance and upkeep on the property, but by denying himself physical rights of occupation has he forfeited his essential right to defend his own territory? It is suggested that occupation still subsists through those rights which the owner has retained and through those obligations which he has specifically accepted. Furthermore, by accepting and demanding management rights and obligations over the let portions of the estate the owner is to a degree still in occupation even though by letting property he has voluntarily curtailed the full extent of his management. However, landlords and tenants are not alone in sharing a property between them: the State is often a third party to their agreements for it sustains by statute a duty to interfere and has distributed some of an owner's rights among other interested parties. In the case, for example, of the letting of property for domestic occupation and in the letting of lands for farming or other trades, the State has regulated the bargain which may be struck between owner and occupier. In some instances this has imposed on the owner conditions which he would not voluntarily accept; and in other instances the State has even granted rights to certain bodies to expropriate the whole of an owner's interest.

Responsibilities

The degree to which an owner may do what he likes with his own must, in any civilised society, be proscribed and rights of expropriation or leasing be given to certain bodies for the exercise of their obligations in the public interest (eg the provision of light, power, sewage disposal, water, roads, etc). Apart from the obligations and duties imposed by law and custom both owner and occupier of land have certain moral responsibilities for good use and management. Professor John Marsh of the University of Reading in a paper entitled *Ethics and their role in the development of future policies for agriculture, land use and related scientific and industrial practice: an economic viewpoint* said:

We need to understand such concepts as good, evil, status, justice, equity, the rights of property and the obligations of the individual to the state if we are to appreciate the forces which bind societies together . . . Those who embark on economics accept that the issue of how society uses resources, merits careful thought. . .

The attempt to treat economics as if it were independent of ethics is . . . doomed to failure . . . To do his job well . . . [the economist] . . . must recognise . . . and make explicit the ethical framework within which he is working. This must take account of the attitudes of other people . . .

The first of these attitudes can be summed up in the word "stewardship". It implies acceptance of a responsibility which is changing and growing but not different in kind from that which many farmers have traditionally seen as their duty to "keep the land in good heart" . . .

The second approach is at variance with traditional views where nature is seen as there for man to use. Many critics of modern farming see the issue in terms of the wonders of nature . . . and the rapaciousness of humanity. This may give rise to a 20th century form of puritanism . . . Its logic must be for minimum agriculture since farming inevitably makes one species thrive at the expense of others . . . There are no weeds, only plants of equal right . . .

Economists are often heard to condemn a policy because it is "inefficient". However what this means is sometimes obscure . . . Markets provide values only for those goods which enter into exchange. Non-traded goods, such as a pleasing landscape, a peaceful society or the sound of the birds may be greatly valued but if a calculation is made in market terms alone a system may seem to be efficient which destroys some or all of these good things. To include non-market elements involves some system of estimating their value in relation to those goods which have a price. We have no simple or unambiguous way of doing this.

There is a great deal in what Professor Marsh has to say and although he was speaking primarily of farming, his points are applicable in large measure to land management and to the attitude of some people, not of the countryside, towards it. Good management springs from the acceptance by the owner of a responsibility, which is his alone and of which he has been aware, in many cases, from his earliest childhood. This responsibility, and its acceptance, is engendered by the fact of ownership of a particular and definable defensible space. The private owner is not anonymous. He cannot escape from his responsibilities; he must accept them.

An estate on which, with varying rights of ownership and occupation, people live and on which many of them depend for their livelihoods is in itself an organism which can grow, diminish and change in accordance with the attitudes of those who live on it. Those attitudes may be positive (actively in favour) or negative (passively against); some may see their participation and interest as contributing to the general good. Behind this perception lies the animal instinct of defensible space; a territorial attachment to the land itself expressed through acts or attitudes within the community which is indeed part of the land; an attitude which is not directly influenced by the legal owner of the estate. Occupiers do not work their land, nor protect their homes, out of devotion to the owner, but out of devotion to the territory. The owner can, however, influence that devotion by his approach to and practice of land management. His decisions and actions must affect the occupier's attitude and commitment to his land. The landowner usually occupies some portion of his estate, but his presence on the estate, his demonstrated interest in it, his management actions on it and his understanding of the property as a single unit, together with his reversionary rights are indeed, as maintained earlier in this chapter, a form of occupation even of those lands which are presently let. This "occupation" is epitomised by good management which is deep and committed enough to show.

Good management

Not all owners, nor all managers necessarily show "good management". What indeed is it? The manager who is acting for the owner is following another's path, but as a professional is not powerless. There are ways of implementing a policy, there are arguments which may be used to change a direction, but in the end good management is the intelligent application of a policy which acknowledges that ownership is divisible; that a landholding is not an impersonal investment because it is territory and territory has people on it. The land is the fundamental good by which life is sustained; the landowner has ultimate control over its development and use. This statement, of course, holds true whoever or whatever the owner may be, from a private individual through trusts and institutions of all types, statutory undertakers, local or regional authorities to the State itself.

The degree of control which an owner may exercise over his land has been prescribed and restricted by the action of the State from time to time and in a few cases the State (or other body acting under the law) has the right to take positive action against an owner's wishes, but, on the whole, control such as that exercised through the planning process is negative. Change of use and the process of development may be prohibited, but other than as briefly mentioned above, it cannot be forced upon a reluctant owner. The spur, or goad to development is an offer of consideration of sufficient weight, in the circumstances, to bias an owner's choice. To some extent, therefore, the landowner is the guardian of the countryside by exercising his right of action and his right to say "no". In doing this, of course, he may be making a personal sacrifice. On the other hand, when he does wish to change a land use or to develop, he cannot do so without public consent.

There are, thus, checks and balances between private and public inclinations and wishes. Certain private proposals may be publicly prohibited; certain public proposals may be privately resisted (not always successfully). Some actions relating to land use are not, yet, within the public sphere and things may be done on the land which are outside the control of anybody except the owner and perhaps the occupier. On the whole, care of the countryside rests upon those who use and own it as it always has. Here is a dichotomy, namely the division between private need and public demand. In this context private need is the need to be able to run an efficient business without interference and public demand is for further control. This demand leans towards the sanitisation, "beautification" and preservation of a countryside which in all essentials has grown only through constant change. The landowner stands often at the point of balance.

Choice

Here there lies a choice epitomised by the private owner between what to do and what not to do. Here lies the essential difference between the effective private owner, who can make a management decision on his own without apparent justification and for a variety of reasons, and the public owner (perhaps the State), who in essence does not exist. The public owner's decisions are taken by an employee, be he the local or national agent, be he chief executive, clerk or minister whose commitment to the land is impersonal, dictated by his position, terms of service and the rules under which he must operate. Such a person may indeed be dedicated and skilful; but his tie is ephemeral, his service proscribed, his eyes perhaps on the next rung of the ladder. With his employment over, his office in other hands, himself in another position he is no longer concerned. He acts always on behalf of an owner who can never be identified, for when the last of the curtains is drawn back in the inner sanctum there is either nobody there (in a true democracy) or a self-seeking dictator.

The actions of the private owner are not, of course, always pure and blameless. They are usually dictated by a variety of needs stemming from his own attitude. A need, say to preserve his land for future generations as far as he is able to, a need to ensure the prosperity of his own landholding and that of his tenants, a need to serve the local inhabitants (of whom he may have a considerable knowledge), a need to serve the population at large and of course a need to satisfy personal preference and choice. These it must be acknowledged may be unappreciated by others: some of them indeed may spring from a misunderstanding of how other people live, but this is a fault in most of us. So we slip back to the territorial imperative: to the hold which territory has over our actions and reactions – the hold which land has on all of us, the need which we have to be able to say "This is mine. This will I defend".

CHAPTER 4

The changing face of landownership

Synopsis
Status of landowner – Change – Rights and obligations – Land, original base of power – A waning influence – Landowner in parliament – Dissipation of power – Widening parliamentary franchise – Depression – First World War – Destruction – Survival – New responsibilities – Attitude of the landowner – Good manager.

Introduction

Before the industrial revolution changed Britain and before, towards the last quarter of the 19th century, cheap food became available from other countries and in particular from the New World, land was a sure source of wealth. The landowner held sway by right and custom over his manor; he could command service and in effect deny freedom to some and by reason of his power his standing was of necessity high. His status, social, economic and political, survived hardly scratched into the middle years of the 19th century and, indeed, it was accepted within the fraternity of the rich that wealth, epitomised by landownership, remained for many years the key to both social and political recognition. During the last century, however, this key began, albeit slowly, to slip out of the hand as pressures, economic and popular, applied by new circumstances and new perceptions, squeezed it out. This was not immediately recognised while it was happening; indeed, it may not have been fully recognised even at the end of the 20th century. It is not so much the landowners who have not recognised the change, but others who cling to their ideas of what the countryside is like and what goes on there.

Power and change

Landowners have confronted change and have been among the first to see and adapt to those conditions which have evolved following the two world wars of this century. Some who hold or aspire to wealth find that a degree of privilege (or the sensation of privilege) may still be bought and position sought through its influence, but no longer is a landholding an essential part of this process. Today, more so than ever before, position and power are ephemeral and are easily lost. There remains a divide between rich and poor, between rulers and ruled whatever the political regime. This chapter tries to show how the spotlight has moved: how the landowner who was once among the powerful by reason of his lands should now claim a position only by example rather than by right.

Some rights and obligations are inherent in the ownership of any asset and where ownership involves the use of the asset (and in the case of land where it may involve occupation) then additional rights and obligations become apparent. Landownership has never been without its rights, but neither has it been without its obligations. Rights and obligations today are different from what they were; indeed, what were sometimes considered rights in the past would today be considered undeserved privileges which have properly been removed.

A waning interest

It is interesting to compare the standing of the present-day landowner with that of his forebears and to trace briefly, and in the barest outline, the changes in the standing and function of the private landowner over the fairly recent past. People have acquired land by being given it (earlier perhaps from a grateful monarch), by buying it, by marrying in to it and by inheriting it (not to forget occasionally by seizing it). The ownership of that land was the ownership of a base from which power could be exercised, because to own a particularly large area of land, gave to the owner local power; but much more than that, it gave the entrée to society and especially to London society and hopefully to Court through which privilege and often political influence flowed. About a century ago, maybe even less, Parliament was largely made up of the landowning classes both in the House of Commons and, of course, in the House of Lords. Anybody who had ambitions to be involved in government could realise those ambitions more easily through the portals of landownership than through virtually any other door.

Mark Girouard in his book *Life in the English Country House*[1] says,

Land . . . however, was little use without one or more country houses on it. Land provided the fuel, a country house was the engine which made it effective . . . it was the headquarters from which the land was administered and power organised. It was a show case from which to exhibit supporters and good connections . . . it was an image maker which projected an aura of glamour . . . around its owner.

Then it all began slowly to crumble away. It is not possible to date the start of this process. Historic and economic events had a hand in it as did the changing social climate and the aspirations and ambitions of other orders of society. Perhaps the first wind of change blew across the English Channel with the French revolution.

Widening of the franchise

However, from the end of the second decade of the 19th century, change in the social structure of Britain was peacefully engineered by a gradual widening of the parliamentary franchise brought about by a recognition that a better educated people must needs have a say in choosing how and by whom the country was to be governed and by an acknowledgement that one sector of society, namely the wealthy and privileged, had no absolute right to govern. This recognition was not swift and probably not expressed in such harsh terms, but the effect over the years was to curtail the power of land, of the landed proprietors and the rising barons of industry who strove to become landowners. Gradually power spread widely across the populace so that nobody was in fact debarred from taking a part in the governance of country, county or district. David Cannadine in his book *The Decline and Fall of the British Aristocracy*[2] says,

Until 1905 every British Cabinet, whether conservative or liberal, was dominated by the traditional territorial classes, with the brief exceptions of the Liberal ministries of 1892-95. But a greater break came with Campbell-

---

1 Girouard, M (1978) *Life in the English Country House* Yale University Press.
2 Cannadine, D (1990) *The Decline and Fall of the British Aristocracy* Yale University Press.

Bannerman's government, after which landowners were usually in the minority. The Asquith administration was slightly more patrician than its predecessor, but Lloyd George . . . gave much less space to them. So, predictably, did Macdonald . . . The Conservative and National governments of the twenties and thirties were much more landed in membership; in 1924 at least half of Baldwin's cabinet could be so described, and in 1937 the aristocratic contingent in Chamberlain's administration was not much less. In both cases this was a presence out of all proportion to their much depleted presence in the Commons and the Lords.

Later he points out that in

1914 23% of Tory MPs boasted landed links, by 1935 the figure was less than 10% . . . At the most generous estimate there were by 1939 only fifty MPs primarily interested in the land. In the Commons as in the countryside, five hundred years of aristocratic history had been reversed in fifty.

The make-up of Parliament since the Second World War clearly demonstrates that representation of the people is by the people, from whatever sector of society they come and that it is temperament and ambition which guide people into politics and no longer tradition, beyond that to which any family is subject, whatever their origins.

Depression and destruction

Throughout much of the 19th century agricultural land continued to occupy a high place in the estimation of investors. The rents to which it gave rise came from a still flourishing agriculture over which the landowners exercised a largely benevolent control, though their tenants at that time were little able to protect themselves from eviction, nor to take out from their farms when they left them, much of what they had over the years put in; but things were changing, agricultural holdings legislation began to curb the near despotism of the landlords. Then a deep agricultural depression hit the country in the last quarter of the 19th century. Farm rents and values fell while the growing prosperity of the towns and of manufacturing and business generally severely lessened the attraction of agricultural land as a secure and worthwhile investment. As the century came to its close, capital in land and in furniture, pictures and objects d'art had in many cases to be realised to reduce a mounting debt among some of the landed establishment. By the 1930s after the

First World War and after another depression in farming, many of the smaller estates had disappeared and many of the larger ones were greatly reduced in size.

The booklet produced in 1973 as part of the exhibition held at the Victoria and Albert Museum in London, *The Destruction of the Country House*, showed that in the previous 100 years 1,124 country houses had been destroyed. In introducing the list the booklet points out that this cannot be called an exhaustive list but that "it is likely to include most of the more important losses of the last hundred years". 1,124 houses recorded as being destroyed by the early 1970s does not mean that the process has ceased; more have gone since and more have been adapted to new uses (conference centres and hotels for example). These figures do not of course mean that an equivalent number of estates has been broken up, though the destruction of the house must have meant disruption of many of the landholdings which those houses almost always complemented.

This dismemberment of landed estates and the shrinkage of the political and economic power which attached to them, was not merely a phenomenon of economics, for it was encouraged by radical governments at the beginning of the century and by the rise at that time of the Labour Party through which the working classes (if that expression must be used) were at last able to have some political voice. That, at the end of the 20th century, there are still many agricultural estates left, both large and small, is almost a matter of some surprise, but despite crippling taxation during and after the Second World War, a surge in land values in the second half of this century, prosperity in agriculture and intelligent administration kept the wastage at bay for a time: the future, which is not the province of this book to predict, remains uncertain even when account is taken of the large reductions in capital taxation recently introduced, for laws can be altered.

Survival of the landed estate

The survival of the landed estate, in so far as it has survived, is perhaps, though unperceived, fortunate for the future welfare of this country, for the attitude of the landowner has undergone a great change in the last 50 years. As privilege and position have been withdrawn there has arisen a new generation of owners, many of whom have come to the hard recognition that landownership, while it can still carry a comfortable life in many cases, is a difficult and demanding business with responsibilities sharply in the public eye.

These responsibilities relate to the land and to all who live upon it, enjoy it and draw their livelihood from it, be they estate tenants, employees or unconnected inhabitants; be they the local population or those who come to visit the countryside from far away. The extent of the landowner's responsibility to all these people cannot be precisely defined but he should be aware of their needs (and sometimes of their demands, reasonable or unreasonable). His own family have also rights and needs and much of the skill of land management rests in being able to reconcile these conflicting aspirations and ambitions. This is a thing which of course cannot be done: for a solution of one problem may well entail the creation of another and the satisfaction of one petitioner (for want of a better word) may be to the detriment of others. The skill lies in ensuring the greatest good to the greatest number, but in the process of land management it must never be forgotten that the countryside is a place of work, that the land is in use for production and that people's livelihoods depend upon its efficient management. Those thousands in the urban world who are encouraged to look upon the countryside as a place of recreation and pleasure, a beautiful landscape, never changing, must needs be instructed in the realities of life and endeavour. With the power over his own lands which is left to him the landowner can exercise immense good, particularly in detail, which an impersonal owner, who may have to manage by the rule book, cannot.

The attitude of the landowner

While it is possible to trace changes in the size and constitution of a landed estate over many years and, thus, to show how estates in general have diminished in area and value since the middle of the last century, it is not easy, in fact may be impossible, to define in any measurable way the attitude of landowners to their estates over a similar period, nor to reckon the efficiency of land management nor its essential drive at any one time; for there is no gauge against which to set these things. When land really was a substantial source of power and prestige the owner's approach to it may have been one of pride in the rightness of things, of security in the firm source of his wealth and of patrician concern for those who worked on his estates as tenants or employees, but this attitude cannot be measured against the way in which the modern landowners regard their property for such a measurement is both unquantifiable and must be affected by the climate of today's thinking.

The good landlord

A person considered a "good" landlord in the 1860s might be thought a "bad" one in the 1990s; just as a "good" landlord in the 1990s might be considered unbalanced from a viewpoint 130 years old. One can perhaps only suggest that the political, economic and social changes which have taken place since 1870 coupled with a growing public awareness of the countryside, a clamour for access and an insistence that the "heritage" belongs to all, have caused today's landowner to adopt a different attitude to his lands from that of his recent predecessors. He is after all a different person who has been reared in a different world from theirs. He may still take personal pride in his inheritance and in his family, but it is a more secret pride and he can hold it only so long as he is prepared to accept the many overt obligations which landownership now must bear. The fact that he is sometimes the last bastion against the overweening power of bureaucracy or against the insistent importuning of the developer may not always be appreciated, but needs stating here at least once. He has obligations, duties, towards a wide variety of people not just because he owns or controls an asset much in the eye of the public but also because he, like the employer and business man in other spheres, must accept that his actions affect many people whom he never sees but who claim an interest in "his" piece of country, as inhabitants at large, as well as those who claim (or demand) rights of unrestricted access to inappropriate places or over land which is in use as the basic ingredient of farming or forestry. The landowner has to weigh different claims against each other, but not less does he have to weigh them against the well-being of those to whom he owes a more compelling duty, namely his tenants.

Very many people who now live in the countryside have no immediate connection with it. They work in the towns and use the towns as their centres but enjoy (and why not?) life out of the towns and have a right to express an opinion about the place in which they live, but, for example, they do not get used to the smells of the countryside and are frequently offended by them. It is often among these well-meaning but ill-informed people that the landowner has to run his estate. He owes a duty to them, as to all his neighbours, but they too owe a duty to the countryside, which many of them have yet to learn must be economically viable as well as visually satisfying.

Land management

Land management also has changed over the years. It used to be easier than it now is. It was a discipline which grew out of stewardship. Charles Curtis wrote the first edition of his book *Estate Management – a practical handbook for landlords, agents and pupils* in 1879. In the preface to that edition he said:

He who intends to qualify himself for such interesting and responsible work . . . must in these days . . . give up the idea that he need only abandon himself to the pleasures of country life and that all needful information will be picked up by the way.

In the preface to the sixth edition in 1911 he said, among other things,

I hope this sixth edition may assist those who are engaged in piloting the land question of Great Britain through its devious and hazardous channels . . . for the estates of England . . . are beset with difficulties which our forefathers never contemplated . . . The aim should be: to induce the land to yield its utmost; to secure to the labourer a living wage and a decent home; and to enable the landowner to live among his people.

Problems there always were, but attitudes change. The well-meant words "to live amongst his people" strike today a false note. Land management at the end of the 20th century is complex as never before. The land and its use are controlled as never before. Central and indeed local government have usurped some of the functions of the owner. He cannot do what he likes with his own (nor can any of us). The land manager has to know and understand many laws and regulations and in the implementation of policy to guide the owner through them. Landownership is a testing discipline. Whatever professional help the owner may call upon, whatever the extent of his interest or of his disinterest, he cannot avoid that ultimate responsibility which is his alone.

CHAPTER 5

Public concern for the countryside

Synopsis
Private property rights and market economy – Social welfare considerations – Analysing resource-allocating transactions – Private property and public goods – Public governance of land use – Dichotomy between town planning and rural planning – Role of private landowners in rural planning – Provision of rural housing for local need – Effect of the urban view on rural environment.

Introduction

This chapter addresses the balance between the exercise and allocation of property rights through the market mechanism and the proper recognition of non-financial values in determining land use. It questions the appropriateness of the exercise of existing statutory controls on land use, arguing that existing controls can be as damaging to the countryside as unrestrained private management.

Private property rights and the market economy

At first sight, the notion that the use of land and buildings should be governed by private property rights of ownership, possession, occupation and use fits comfortably with a market economy. However, individuals or organisations who own or occupy land and buildings make decisions concerning their use which affect others, intentionally or unintentionally, directly or indirectly. If, as a result of such decisions, everyone so affected becomes better off or, at least, not worse off, none has cause for complaint. If, on the other hand, in the process of some people becoming better off others perceive themselves to be worse off, the latter may believe that they have cause to claim that their own individual rights have been infringed and that in the process they have to bear an unwarranted cost.

The individuals made worse off may have no legal relationship with the author of the decision which gave rise to their loss and, therefore, no contractual redress against the decision maker. The common law mechanism for dealing with such losses is the law of tort, which is directly and intimately concerned with harmful acts which result in measurable damage. In the case of land, the torts of trespass, nuisance, negligence and the rule in *Rylands* v *Fletcher* are particularly relevant. They operate, in relation to land and buildings, on the premise that the use of property should be conducted in such a way that it does not cause interference with others. Or, put the other way round, enables those who have suffered trespass or damage to their property, to seek redress through the courts for restitution of the damage they have sustained. In the main, however, such mechanisms are expensive to exercise and are based on individual injury or damage. They are generally inappropriate for the restitution of damage to society as a whole.

Social welfare considerations

A use (or transaction) which produces a profile of costs and benefits which is efficient from the point of view of the direct participants may not be efficient from the point of view of society as a whole. Use which involves a reallocation of resources will be socially efficient if there are no external costs or benefits or if all the consequences of a particular reallocation are taken fully into account by the participants. In a free-market economy individuals only attempt to maximise their own private utility or profit, and external costs and benefits will not be reflected in the price of things. In short, it is full social costs which are important in determining an efficient resource allocation and private costs which determine prices (Bannock *et al* 1987)[1]. Political economy (or welfare economics) is concerned with the ordering of the economic behaviour of individuals in a manner which achieves, in addition to private benefit, the greatest efficiency at a social level of resource allocation. It aims to identify behaviour which may be considered to be socially inefficient and to prescribe corrective solutions.

Solutions which are intended to modify the economic behaviour of individuals may require the support, either directly or indirectly,

---

1 Bannock, G, Baxter, RF and Davis, E (1987) *Dictionary of Economics* 4th ed, Hutchinson, London.

of legal authority. Although market inefficiency may result from many imperfections, external costs (uncompensated losses that are imposed on individuals or firms by some harmful activity) are most likely to give rise to legal intervention in the operation of the market. Coase (1960)[1] demonstrated that perfectly competitive markets could, in principle, control harmful activities efficiently. If, for example, the law required a firm to compensate the victims of its pollution for the harm it imposed on them, the firm would continue to pollute up to the point at which the profit from an increment of pollution is exceeded by the increased compensation payment. The point at which all the profit from an increment of pollution has to be paid to the victims as compensation may be considered to represent a socially acceptable level of harm. At this point the firm should cease to increase the levels of pollution.

This analysis relies, however, on several simplifying assumptions, notably that: there is a direct and unambiguous chain of causation between the pollution and the damage; the polluter and "victim" are aware that pollution is occurring; the polluter and victim can be identified; an appropriate form of compensation can be agreed; and that the cost of imposing the compensation is zero. Transaction costs, which include the costs of obtaining information and of searching, negotiating and enforcing agreements are seldom, if ever, zero. They may, indeed, be so high in relation to the value of the resources involved that they completely frustrate a market solution to the problem.

In such circumstances the law can establish and define legal rights to clarify the basis upon which the bargaining process should operate. However, the limitations of the free market in taking full account of external costs has led to different approaches to the analysis of transactions which focus on the manner in which transactions are effected and organised.

Analysing resource-allocating transactions

The market approach pays little attention to transaction costs while the alternative (or highly modified) approach to transaction analysis arises from a presumption that attempts on the part of those

---

1 Coase, R (1960) "The Problem of Social Cost", Journal of Law and Economics 3: 1–44.

involved in the process of resource utilisation to economise on transaction costs can play a major part in explaining resource allocations in circumstances in which the market mechanism fails. Such approaches have been referred to as "neo-institutional" (Burrows and Veljanovski 1981)[1]. "Institutional" in this sense may be taken to mean the rules governing the process of exchange and the mechanisms developed to give effect to these rules. It develops a more complex, conceptual picture of the economic and non-economic factors relevant to broader (legal/institutional) analysis of resource allocation.

In attempting to integrate behavioral aspects of resource allocation with economic and legal models it tends, as a consequence, to be less elegant and less precise than market-based models. In some respects it is the antithesis of more conventional market analysis: rather than focusing on (market) equilibrium analysis, it presumes that "inefficiency" gives rise to adaptive efforts to minimise costs. It places emphasis instead on the adaptation of participants in the exchange process to disequilibrium. Rather than verify an efficiency-type hypothesis, it identifies legal and institutional phenomena and uses them to develop conceptual categories of "market" behaviour. In contrast to the free market concept of "efficiency" in which individual transactions should conform to the predictions of perfect competition, efficiency in institutional terms is concerned with adjusting to an ambiguous, uncertain and changing environment.

If transaction costs are exacerbated by the extent of the imperfection of the markets to which they relate, this is likely to encourage opportunism. Efforts to realise individual gains through lack of candour or honesty in transactions gives rise to the need for some form of governance that will discourage parties from being opportunistic. This is not to say, however, that the "law" should imply terms that the parties might have agreed to had they addressed the problem at the contract formation stage. It is, rather, to argue for the provision of an "adjustment" process to preserve continuing contractual relations in the face of opportunism and deal with cases where contracts are incompletely specified. There is always a possibility that latent (and often unobservable) categories

---

1 Burrows, P and Veljanovski, CG (1981) *The Economic Approach to Law* Butterworths, London.

of transaction cost may be used to justify observed or expected outcomes. The "neo-institutional" approach is particularly susceptible to this criticism. It relies heavily on the rigour and discipline applied to any consideration of transaction costs both in theoretical discussions and in the interpretation of institutional phenomena.

Private property and public goods

A further complication arising from the allocation of resources resulting from the exercise of private property rights concerns the extent to which land should be considered to be a private or a public commodity. Economists distinguish between private and public goods according to three main criteria, namely non-exclusive, non-rival, incapable of being rejected. Applied to land and buildings, they are non-exclusive if it is impossible to restrict others from using them; non-rival if one person's use of them does not deprive others from using them; and cannot be rejected if individuals cannot abstain from their consumption even if they wanted to (Bannock *et al* 1987)[1].

A distinction should be made between a public good, as defined by economists, and public use of land, which may or may not accommodate the provision of a public good: land used for a public highway is a public use accommodating a public good although a right of way across privately owned land may also be a public good. Land and buildings often accommodate public uses although the land and buildings themselves may be privately owned or owned by a public body. Equally, they may be owned by a public body but put to private use. There is a vogue for claiming that land, particularly countryside and coast, is part of the collective heritage of the nation and should, therefore, be treated as a public good. There is little or no legal justification for this vogue, but it has popular appeal and is only likely to become acceptable if these views were strong enough to be achieve real recognition by policy makers.

---

1 Bannock, G, Baxter, RF and Davis E (1987) *Dictionary of Economics* 4th ed, Hutchinson, London.

Public governance of land use

The past 100 years or so has produced a steady and marked increase in the extent to which the ownership, occupation and use of land and buildings has been affected by social and political influences. One may say, simplistically, that this has been necessary to overcome the inadequacies of the market mechanism in dealing with the allocation of land and buildings, representing, as they do, a most imperfect genus of commodities in a most imperfect genus of markets. Equally important, however, is the change in the institutional framework governing the use and development of land. The changes which occurred from the point of view of the role and power of landowners are considered in other chapters. The most marked change in the governance of land use by those not owning property rights has been the development of the system of town and country planning. Curiously, although the terms "town" and "country" are explicitly linked together in general terminology, the main impetus for this form of governance at the local authority level of policy making was and continues to be the governance of urban areas. As a general rule, this framework of governance has been achieved without recourse to the acquisition of property rights by the power of statute. The alternative approach involving the expropriation of property rights, land nationalisation in one form or other, has never gained widespread support.

Town planning gained distinct professional recognition in Britain in 1914 with the creation of the Town Planning Institute, which initially drew most of its membership from the Royal Institute of British Architects and the Royal Institution of Chartered Surveyors. Town planning only gained its "country" suffix in 1942 when the Ministry of Works and Planning became the Ministry of Town and Country Planning. The Ministry of Works and Planning commissioned a study of land utilisation in rural areas which resulted in the publication of the Scott Report in 1942 (Report of the Committee on *Land Utilisation in Rural Areas*. Cmnd 6378 HMSO). Subsequently, the next major piece of legislation dealing with planning was entitled the Town and Country Planning Act 1947.

Town and country planning became entangled with the broad development of the Welfare State. This may be attributable to a variety of influences including: the public health origins of town planning, subsequently translated into a concern for the environmental quality of urban areas; the 20th-century demand for access to the countryside; and the need for urgent reconstruction of the industrial and residential fabric of the nation after the Second World War. However, the linking of "town" and "country" implies a degree of integration between the two which is misleading. Fear of uncontrolled urban expansion led policy makers to seize on the countryside as the beach-head for containing urban sprawl. There was no serious intention to plan the countryside in the way that towns were planned. The most significant policies with regard to rural planning were that farming and forestry interests would look after the rural environment, rural economy and rural community issues and that, in other respects, the countryside should be considered as the playground of the urban community. The countryside became a *cordon sanitaire* around urban areas.

The dichotomy between town planning and rural planning

The dichotomy between town planning and country planning still exists at the government level and at the operational level of property management. Town planning now lies largely under the governance of the Department of the Environment; "rural" planning (there is really no generic equivalent to "town" corresponding to the countryside) was, for at least the decades of the 1950s, 1960s and 1970s, essentially under the governance of the Ministry of Agriculture, Fisheries and Food. The Ministry of Agriculture still remains a powerful force, but no longer the dominant influence it once represented. At this constitutional level of policy making the institutional pattern of governance is fragmented. At the operational level of day to day decision making, the pattern of land ownership and occupation is also fragmented.

In the rapid development of town planning post 1947 the profession earned for itself a reputation for being a profession based largely on ideology. In a critique of town planning Foley (1960)[1] explains that:

the ideology of town planning provides a philosophic basis for the activity. It indicates the main goals and approaches. The ideology provides a basic

---

1 Foley, DL (1960) "British Town Planning: One Ideology or Three?", *British Journal of Sociology* 11: 211.

operating rationale. In simplified terms it defines the situation for its participants, particularly specifying the main kinds of problems that the activity is to tackle and the major types of solutions, and the spirit of their application. It characteristically includes a defensive tone, providing the simple replies to criticism or attacks. While town planning also has been developing a sub-culture that specifies in richer detail the behaviour to be expected in varied situations, the ideology stresses the major ideas and approaches.

An ideology tends to build around seemingly self-evident truths and values and, in turn, to bestow a self-justifying tone to its main propositions and chains of reasoning. While the ideology may well contain highly rational arguments, it is characteristically ultra-rational in its overall spirit. It becomes comfortable and protective: and in this way contributes to the emotional security of the participant and to his self-confidence in carrying out the activity. While the ideology thus provides an essential kind of consensus supporting the activity, its self-evident and self-justifying nature may also contribute to a smug and traditional outlook and discourage a healthy self-awareness and sceptical re-examination. Foley depicts town planning as part of a broader social programme,

. . . responsible for providing the physical basis for better urban community life; the main ideals toward which town planning is to strive are (a) the provision of low-density residential areas (b) the fostering of community life (c) the control of conurban growth. The main task of town planning is to reconcile competing claims for the use of limited land so as to provide a consistent, balanced and orderly arrangement of land uses: its central function to provide a good (or better) physical environment; a physical environment of such quality is essential for the promotion of a healthy and civilised life.

(Foley 1960)

Foley's suggestion highlights the overwhelming preoccupation with "towns" within the British planning system. There is a marked divergence of philosophy between town planning and "country" planning. The former relies on a presumption that "development" is almost a state of nature in land use terms; the main concern is its form and distribution. In the post-war evolution of town and country planning, the general trend has been to focus on urban planning, creating a built environment appropriate for an essentially urban economy and urban society. Town and country planners have identified policies which separated rural from urban which may be expressed generally as a policy of "urban containment". The process of urban containment, based as it must be on an implicit assumption that urban areas are capable of being self-sustaining, involves carrying out development within urban areas to cater for that economy and community while preserving rural villages. Policies that have been introduced to fortify urban containment include: green belts; urban regeneration; development of new towns; and strict planning restrictions in the rural areas. Conversely, country planning appears to presume that "development" in the countryside is largely inappropriate and should be resisted wherever possible, unless it is for agriculture or forestry (in which case it is probably acceptable). The main emphases in country planning appear to be: (i) to resist the conversion of countryside to "urban" use (whatever "urban" means); and (ii) to maintain the landscape value of the countryside (implicitly for the primary benefit of the urban or ex-urban population).

The political justification of town and country planning was severely attacked during the reign of the Thatcher government. Planning was seen by government as a facilitating mechanism to support the market system in allocating resources. Nevertheless, the primary division between town planning and country planning remained. Indeed, the move toward market-led development served to increase the pressure on rural areas to resist urban encroachment. The extent of the weakness of the town and country planning system in safeguarding the physical environment of the countryside, let alone facilitating the development of the rural economy and rural communities is demonstrated by the claim that "planning" has no more influence over development in the countryside than other environmental controls such as building regulations, public health regulations and highway regulations.

There are countless examples of development in the countryside, primarily intended to support either local urban communities or the economic welfare of the general population centred as it is in towns, which has had a detrimental effect on rural communities and the appearance of the countryside. Examples include: waste disposal plants; refuse tips; "out-of-town" shopping centres; and the constant development and enhancement of the roads infrastructure. The level of degradation to the rural environment created by the scale and intrusive impact of such developments should not be belittled by discussion of the statistics of the conversion of land use from what is loosely described as "rural" to what is equally loosely defined as "urban".

The scale of development characteristically encountered in rural communities almost pales into insignificance when compared with urban intrusions into the countryside, yet the level of detailed criticism to which they are subjected is out of all proportion to the lasting impact which they are likely to generate. Furthermore, the most intrusive developments are often accompanied either by a compulsory expropriation of the property rights necessary to achieve the development (most notably highway schemes and schemes sponsored by statutory undertakers) or, in the case of large-scale commercial developments, a change of ownership from owners who may be considered as part of the rural community to those who are considered to be that part of the urban development community constantly on the look-out for green-field sites for new development.

The role of private landowners in rural planning

When it comes to the more positive aspects of protecting and safeguarding the countryside heavy reliance is still placed on private owners and occupiers of land to support and sustain the rural economy and to protect and conserve the landscape and environmental quality of the countryside. At the national level the preservation of the natural environment is the overwhelming determinant of countryside planning. However, financial acknowledgement of the proper fulfilment of this responsibility is so deficient that at points of pressure, where commercial values overwhelm social values, the British system of country planning relies heavily on private organisations such as the National Trust, the Royal Society for the Protection of Birds, the Woodland Trust and local conservation trusts, to raise the cash to acquire property rights to ensure conservation of landscape; habitat or heritage.

This is not only a waste of resources (acquiring the entire bundle of property rights to prevent the exercise of development rights in a manner which is financially irrational) but it highlights the limitations of the market mechanism in fully reflecting the value of non-use benefits. Reliance is also placed on landowners to do what they can to support rural communities as well as the rural economy, though at the same time they are mistrusted to do so without profiteering. In fact landowners face not only planning policies primarily determined from an urban perspective, they face other policies determined primarily with the interests of the urban community in mind. A notable example of this relates to the control of residential property, particularly the leasehold reform legislation of 1967 and 1993 (this will be referred to below).

The resistance to permitted development in rural areas had the effect of increasing the value premium between land in agricultural use and land for development. Converting land from a rural use to an urban use gives rise to a substantial enhancement in its cash value. The mere prospect of such a windfall premium gives rise to enhanced value, referred to as hope value, based on potential use discounted to reflect the likelihood of the conversion being achieved. Ironically, the hope value which arises from land use policy makes planners sceptical of the motives of rural landowners seeking any form of development almost irrespective of its social benefit, for example, affordable housing for local need. This creates a recipe for stagnation of rural communities and economies: planners tend to resist much development in the countryside, implicitly on the basis that the motivation is profit-taking. This discourages landowners from advancing development proposals, however modest, which may be socially or economically beneficial for rural communities if there is any risk that the landowner may receive any surplus over and above the cost of development.

Provision of rural housing for local need

At a time when the rural economy is itself under pressure from the price reforms within agriculture, the pressures on rural communities are acute. Restrictive interpretation of policies enabling rural development to occur fail to take proper account of the operational difficulties faced by socially motivated developers of rural housing for local people, notably housing associations and private landowners. Several reports highlight the problem, most notably a report entitled *The Problems in Rural Areas*, an inquiry chaired by the Duke of Westminster, published in September 1992.

The report identifies the shortage of low cost housing as the most pressing social problem in rural areas. Competing demand from wealthier outsiders, along with a tightening of development control, have been recognised as a dominant feature throughout rural

England. The example of providing housing for local need in rural areas highlights some of the difficulties created by restrictive planning policies applied by district planning authorities in many rural areas despite government guidance to facilitate planning permission for rural housing. For the most part, those groups whose housing needs deserve priority are well defined in the Department of the Environment's Planning Policy Guidance note number 3 (PPG 3) – *Land for Housing*:

(i)   Existing residents needing separate accommodation (newly married couples, people leaving tied accommodation or retirement);
(ii) People whose work provides important services and who need or wish to live close to the local community;
(iii) People who are not necessarily resident locally but have long-standing links with the local community (eg elderly people wishing to move back to a village to be near relatives);
(iv) People with the offer of a job in the locality, who cannot take up the offer because of lack of affordable housing.

During the 19th century virtually all English villages were organised around a similar system of work and lifestyle. Agriculture dominated the lives of the inhabitants, apart from the few that were usually involved in some service and ancillary work. The village typically formed an occupational community, the type of occupational community also seen in industrial areas associated with, for example, shipbuilding and mining. Farm and estate workers typically lived in property which they neither owned nor rented. It was provided by their employer and tied to their employment. Hobsdawm and Rude (1969)[1] suggested that

it is doubtful whether the ownership of land mattered very much to the labourers themselves, who certainly owned none and demanded none. From their point of view the presence or absence of the local squire or gentry might have been more relevant.

During the 20th century the decline of rural employment opportunities began to change the traditional structure. Many inhabitants of the countryside, particularly the young, failing to see good employment prospects in the rural economy, moved from land

---

1 Hobsdawm, EJ and Rude, G (1969) *Captain Swing* Lawrence & Wishart, London.

based employment to find work in the towns. The housing which was released was often considered by the farm or estate owner to be surplus to requirements. Selling the freehold released capital which could be reinvested in the main enterprise. The vacant cottages were sought after by urban residents seeking retirement or second, holiday homes in the countryside. This process began to undermine the village as an occupational community and the working class subculture geared to the needs of the local farm or estate. Landowners had not just been farmers but had also been the pinnacle of the social system.

Research into the social structure of farming communities in East Anglia found the

paramount feeling amongst most of the farmers we interviewed was that a harmonious and well ordered village community had recently been disrupted, or was threatened with disruption, by the arrival of urbanite newcomers.

(Newby *et al* 1978)[1]

The study goes on to emphasise the fact that as the "urbanite newcomers" came to the rural settlements, the resident workers and landowners became more strongly tied together by their local connections. This did nothing for relations between the locals and newcomers. Many farmers saw themselves as being overwhelmed and as one of the farmers interviewed by Newby *et al* clearly expressed:

they get on committees and run them and try to override people who have been here all their lives. There's too many do-gooders who don't understand the country way of life. They try to run the whole show instead of the locals who know all of the ways of the countryside.

Not only did newcomers acquire property in the country, they insinuated themselves into the institutional structure of rural communities.

Four of the distinguishing modern characteristics of rural housing in England are: higher proportions of owner-occupied housing; higher proportions of private rented housing; lower levels of council or housing association housing; a significant proportion of houses

---

1 Newby, H, Bell, C, Rose, D and Saunders, P (1978) *Property Paternalism and Power: Class and Control in Rural England*, Hutchinson, London.

owned as second homes or holiday homes. Since the decline of local authorities as a provider of housing in rural areas, the only group who may possess the desire to develop local housing for motives other than profit are housing associations and private landowners. In either case, however, there is a danger that housing originally built for local people will find its way onto the open market. The process by which this may occur differs in each case and the differences illustrate some of the non-planning impediments to sustainable rural development.

Housing associations, taking this example first, are able to offer subsidised housing to occupants primarily because they are able to obtain funding from a quasi-governmental organisation called the Housing Corporation. They are able to offer the accommodation which they build on one of two bases. The first is to rent it to a tenant. The second is to share the *equity* (or capital cost) with the occupant. In the latter case the occupant provides some capital himself and pays a rent charge to the housing association to cover the remaining proportion of the cost. Under the terms for shared equity schemes, determined by the Housing Corporations, the occupant has the right to "staircase" his own equity in the property up to 100%, at which point he becomes the freehold owner. As the freehold owner he is free to dispose of his own freehold and has every incentive to do so to the highest bidder (not necessarily a local owner). Shared equity schemes are attractive to housing associations because staircasing enables them to recoup the cost of the development and reinvest it into new schemes.

The planning consent under which the development occurred may have included a voluntary agreement with the developer (in this case the housing association) under section 106 of the Planning and Compensation Act 1991 that the accommodation will be for local people. If the first tenant acquires the freehold (by staircasing) and then sells to a non-local, the planning authority is faced with great difficulty in enforcing the section 106 agreement. There is little which the original developer can do to enforce the condition; the planning authority, in pursuing enforcement proceedings, has to obtain an order for possession from the county court. This in itself is not easy, but even if the authority obtains possession it is likely to have to compensate the owner for the price of the house; it then has to find a local purchaser or tenant and in neither case is it likely to recover the full open market price. So, although it may be technically possible to take action to enforce the section 106 agreement to local occupancy of the property, practically it is likely to be ineffective.

A private landowner who wishes to retain the freehold ownership of new housing (to retain control over such matters as local occupancy) may welcome a section 106 agreement limiting occupancy to locals. Nevertheless, the problem of funding the development from unsubsidised sources remains. The owner may either let the property to a local tenant at a statutory fair rent (but which is unlikely to cover the loan charges attributable the cost of construction) or seek a capital premium for the lease in return for a long lease at a low rent. However, the Leasehold Reform Act 1967 and its reinforcement, the Housing and Urban Development Act 1993 (both enacted primarily with urban property in mind), are designed to enable tenants of residential property on a long lease at a low rent to purchase the freehold interest. They are then free to dispose of the freehold as they see fit and although conditions may be attached to the property, they are unlikely to be enforced by the planning authority.

Thus, there is a real risk that, despite the willingness of a local planning authority and a developer in the form of a housing association or private landowner to impose local occupancy conditions on rural housing permissions, other mechanisms – for example the funding conditions for housing association developments or the tenure restrictions on private landowners – will conspire to thwart the condition; to enable the accommodation to find its way into the open rather than "locals only" market to the detriment of the local rural community.

The effect of the urban view on the rural environment

There is a sense that the urban view of the rural environment encourages a kind of suspended animation in which the countryside operates as a green lung for the urban corpus of the nation and a source of relaxation and leisure. This bucolic view denies the countryside the dynamic self-determination which maintains its quality and vitality.

The levels of action at which the institutions with a stake in the countryside operate include the constitutional level, the organisational level and the operational level. At the constitutional level, the legislative framework is dominated by urban issues. At the organisational level of the local planning authority, the urban perspective remains powerful, reinforced by a suspicion that any change of use which allows built development gives rise to profiteering at the expense of the countryside. At the operational level, the combination of increasingly restrictive attitudes governing the freedom of management of rural resources coupled with reward and incentive systems which are inadequate to foster the values commonly associated with the countryside (yet which remain undervalued by the market system) and a confusing mishmash of control policies (which are powerful enough to control urban problems but too insensitive for rural problems) produce such mixed messages to the owners of property rights in rural areas that the pressures on the rural environment remain largely unaddressed. Over the course of the last 50 years or so, we have acquired a framework of control over the use and development of land by institutions without property rights and without a clear set of values by which their perception of "most appropriate" use of land may be accurately gauged.

CHAPTER 6

Estate economy

Synopsis
Value, interest of Crown – Property rights and values – Decision making – Best use of land – Social mix – Ownership and occupation distinguished – Possible co-operation – Rents and their function – Owner as entrepreneur – Choice – Public's interest – Economic management – Holistic management.

What is value?

The study of economy (the administration of the material resources of an individual, community or country) is important in trying to understand the actions and reactions of those who own and occupy land. This chapter is closely concerned with the applied economics of landownership and some of it deals with land values, as do other parts of this book. It is usual and convenient to write and think of land, in all its forms, as having value, but it is not strictly accurate, for what has monetary value is not the land itself but the rights which ownership holds in land. It is only because man can use land that there is any value in it. Ownership, of course, can be and is split. The bundle of rights in the freeholder's hands may be disposed of in part or in its entirety; split by his decision or taken from him by statute and distributed to others. These rights have monetary value. In many cases the capital value of an interest in land is calculated by the valuer at so many times the income to which it is deemed to be capable of giving rise, value in such cases being clearly related to use; thus, perhaps, "no income no value".

The Crown is the ultimate owner of the land, holding those residual rights which underlie all others and the Crown, through Parliament, has in effect the power to override those rights which it long since dispersed; yet these residual rights either have no value because they are not saleable or they hold, in limbo, the total value of all those rights which are capable of rescindment, yet no immediate value is placed upon the Crown's interest; but, from tenants-in-chief downwards ownership has carried rights and those rights have had a value. The freeholder's rights or what in any given case remains of them and the lesser owner's rights in the same land, all have value and as the former's lessen so do the latter's increase. This statement, which can be questioned of course, can lead to the suggestion that full value cannot be easily destroyed, only dissipated; perhaps increased, perhaps lessened by the exercise of those residual rights held by the Crown. That the acquisition by compulsion of full rights over a piece of land, needed, for example, for a motorway, reduces the value of the vendor's interest in land and increases that of the acquiring authority is not in question. The amount of the increase will not necessarily be co-incident with the amount of the loss. The difference in value between the vendor's loss and the acquiror's gain is because of the ability of the new owner (the State, ultimately the Crown) to make a decision on land use; it has nothing to do with the land itself. In the private sphere the value of an interest in land acquired by a purchaser is its value to him (or should be if the vendor negotiates aright). In the public sphere compensation is based upon the vendor's loss, not the public's gain, as perhaps it must be.

The decision maker

Professor Donald Denman writing in *Walmsley's Rural Estate Management* (5th ed) about the economics of rural landownership says,

What is done [on or with land] requires someone to make a decision. In the real world that someone can only be he who has the power to decide and to carry out the decisions made. When we ask who that person might be we are faced with the startling fact that it is not the land itself which is of critical importance to the active world of land ownership economics, but the property right in the land which gives the power to decide how the land shall be used as a factor of production. Property right is the foundation stone upon which the entire framework of landownership rests.

Best use

The aim of the landowner in managing his estate, be it large or small, should be to put the assets of which it is made up to the best use. These assets include land and buildings adapted to farming or horticulture, houses and cottages, gardens and parkland, villages and shops, hotels and garages, water, rivers, wastes and commons together with imponderable business opportunities of which the landowner and others may or may not be aware. What is the best use of those assets?

It is in the nature of ownership that best use does not necessarily mean the most financially profitable use, for, while the ownership of a landed estate is the ownership of a complex business, it is a single business unlike any others. The average business, be it a single undertaking or an amalgam of many, is not really concerned with the "best use" of its assets because that best use must be to ensure the maximisation of profits within the law and within the confines of civilised behaviour: whereas to the landowner a "best use" may in some instances be to use the estate's assets gently with circumspection to enhance or maintain the landscape, or to preserve the architectural merits of a village or the accessibility of land to the general public. So the "best use" may be one for persons other than the owner and sometimes for persons unidentifiable as individuals (the nation at large perhaps?).

While the estate must employ resources for its own use and benefit, it will not necessarily exploit them to the fullest possible extent, for it has, at the same time, to provide non-monetary goods and services for the benefit of others which are not capable of measurement in financial terms. It has, for example, a duty to see that public footpaths and bridleways over estate lands are useable and to ensure that estate tenants over whose land these paths run are aware of their responsibilities towards them. Best use in this respect will probably lessen the value of those holdings which are subject to public rights, but this must be accepted by owner and occupier alike: however, in some areas the demand for public access is so strong that special rights may be granted by the landowner to local inhabitants or indeed to others for payment. Such a voluntary dissipation of rights may be properly rewarded and, while it is not normally a well-spring of profit, it is an action which establishes the owner's position in the public's mind and could even emphasise that someone has to pay to maintain an amenity.

The stronger the demand for a facility the more will people be willing to pay for it and the estate profit from it. However, not all is profit and in judging land management account should be taken of the occasions upon which the owner has, for non-financial reasons, foregone opportunities for development and use. There are some things an owner will not do, actions he will not take, which are imposed by his own preferences or prejudices which are of no benefit to anybody but himself; there may be others of which the local inhabitants are unaware which are at the same time of benefit to them, such as the refusal of a landowner to grant access across estate land to make possible disruptive development elsewhere. This negative action, this refusal, may well affect both estate income and capital, but it is neither recorded nor accounted for.

The letting of rights in land

The business and the well-being of the estate is the use of land by the owner or by a variety of occupiers. In letting land for others to use the owner has leased his own rights of occupation in exchange for money and has awarded to others a degree of ownership equivalent to that which he has himself given up. Where there was one owner there are now two or more, all holding an ownership unit which must be used and managed. The degree of ownership of each is, of course, not the same and the person whom we have been wont to call the "owner" holds the freehold reversion; but the more distant that lies in the future the less the "owner" is regarded. Hence the ease with which governments of all persuasions, without endangering their political futures, enfranchise leaseholds.

In the domestic sphere the letting of houses and cottages is not merely an economic exercise, particularly for the conscientious owner who is anxious to maintain, or indeed to create, a social mix. The nature of the village has changed and continues to do so. Where it originally housed those who worked on the land or were directly employed by the owner, today the number of workers in farming and forestry has shrunk and continues to shrink; some cottages and houses in the village or on the farms are, therefore, no longer wanted for their original purpose. The landowner must balance the needs of the local community with the demand for housing from other sectors of the population and decide what to sell, what to let and what to retain for foreseeable estate use. In doing this he may to an extent be able to control the group mix in order to maintain life within the society. A village consisting, as it has been put, of "royalty and peasants" is in division, if not conflict.

The uses to which the landed estate may be put may be business or domestic and where a decision has been taken to permit a particular use the owner will either split his ownership (as mentioned above) or retain it fully for himself, which infers that he will remain both owner and occupier. In doing this (retaining full ownership) he will have to pay for his occupation by foregoing rent, which will be replaced in the domestic market by the joys of occupation and in the commercial market, by profits. To maintain an understanding from the ownership point of view such rent should be shown in the books as income balanced on the other side by the equivalent "owner's drawings" or by an expense of the trade.

Distinction between ownership and occupation

In the process of owning or managing land it is essential to distinguish between ownership and occupation, for to own and to occupy are two different functions even when they are undertaken by the same person. Ownership takes the long view, balancing present needs against future prospects. What is right for the present occupier and for his immediate business is not necessarily right for the owner nor for a future occupier whose needs, though unquantifiable, cannot be entirely ignored. The present occupier is looking at today's market and at the extent of demand for his products. His investment, therefore, tends to be short-term and the fixed equipment and machinery which he buys to meet his current needs may well have an economic life shorter than its physical life and he will have to write off expenditure accordingly. An owner, on the other hand, asked by his tenant to provide fixed equipment will tend to look at the longer term, at the physical rather than the economic life of the works, in order to satisfy himself, if he can, that what he is asked to provide is suitable for use throughout its physical life. If he cannot be so satisfied he will at least require a rent which is enough to amortise his costs over the economic life of the improvement: more likely, however, he will leave it to the tenant to undertake the expenditure.

Owner and occupier, while both of necessity concerned with the well-being of the occupier's business, may be in conflict over some matters, each having a somewhat different viewpoint. Where the owner is also the occupier he may from time to time find himself as owner in conflict with himself as occupier. Of course an owner who has let land for another's business use is concerned that the occupier shall succeed, for from such success his own welfare and that of the estate will flow. Rents cannot be maintained from failing businesses and it is in his own interests that the owner should encourage the occupier. There may be scope here for special and continuing co-operation between landowner and land occupier, the former perhaps providing information and services usually thought of as outside his remit. In this connection also it is possible that neighbouring estates under different owners would benefit by co-operating through the formation of a larger scale enterprise than either of them could provide on their own. Forestry work and woodlands management, for example, could often be more effectively and cheaply undertaken by two estates together than by each of them apart.

The place of rent

In exchange for land occupation the owner takes rent which he intends to convert into other goods and services for his own use, but that rent must be enough to cover a number of different needs. At the very least the rent must be sufficient to enable the owner to fulfil his obligations under the lease, even if after doing so there is little or nothing left. If, however, rents can do no more than this the estate will fail in the end, for, in the longer term, rents must be high enough to provide for the replacement of fixed equipment as well as yielding a fair return on capital; but here, as far as agricultural property is concerned, is deep water, for what, at any particular time, is a "fair" rent?

Over many years, certainly well back into the last century, let agricultural land has yielded a return on capital of between 1% and 2% (that is after taking account of what the owner has to spend on upkeep and management – often some 40% of the gross rental income). Is this currently a "fair" return on capital? In trying to answer this question certain points must be borne in mind. First, perhaps, the indestructibility of land, its permanence, its ability, in the last analysis, to provide sustenance: second, its tendency to retain its value over the long term (and of course for many years since the end of the Second World War to increase in value above the rate of inflation): third, its ability to hold man's love – the territorial imperative mentioned previously. But are these imponderables, these rather misty attributes really enough to make up for the fact that capital added to the land by way of buildings and works, wears out and needs replacing and that such replacement has not in most cases been funded from accumulated rents but from sales of other, perhaps un-needed land and buildings? This is a process which must surely come to an end at some time.

In facing this question there is the need to recognise the difference between land and capital added to land. The rent of a fully equipped farm reflects three things (or should do), namely:

(a) the agricultural value of the productive farm land, including any quotas added to the farm and any rights to subsidies;

(b) the added value of the fixed equipment (related of course to its contribution to the farming business) together with the value to the farming business of the farm-occupied cottages; and

(c) the predominately residential value of the farmhouse.

If rents could be subdivided like this (not an easy task) the returns on the different elements of the total capital value might well be different from each other. What contribution does the fixed equipment make to the capital value of land? What contribution does the farmhouse make, what contribution the cottages? What contribution, indeed, does the location of the holding itself make to the whole and how far does this factor derive from personal preference or agricultural bias? And what of the nearness to markets, the excellence of communications or the proximity of good theatres and concert halls?

These are no doubt academic questions, but they are questions which emphasise the fact that, unlike ordinary shares in a thriving public company, no piece of land and no holding is exactly like any other. Each may carry unique attractions and disadvantages.

The owner as entrepreneur

In considering all these points an owner may hesitate and be tempted perhaps not to let land but act as an entrepreneur in his own right, to seize and exploit the business opportunity. There is no reason why he should not do so providing that he fully understands what he is doing and appreciates the risks and difficulties involved. Not only must he find or borrow the necessary capital, but he must also distinguish between that required as fixed, long-term capital (financed possibly from a negotiated long loan) and that required as working capital which will fluctuate during the trading year. In making these calculations it is easy for the tyro to underestimate the sums required and for the careful to be too timid. The prospective entrepreneur must also be satisfied with his own ability to manage and to devote himself to the new business or, more importantly perhaps in the present context, to be assured of the ability of whoever he may appoint to do the job for him. Employees as managers may be dedicated, but are human and some may not be of the metal to work to the exclusion of their own enjoyment to establish a business for someone else.

The new business should have every prospect of breaking even within a short time and, within a measurable period, of yielding a positive income, which will include a straight return on capital equivalent to the average safe yield of the day, an allowance or reward for risk, enough to meet the rent for the premises equal to that obtainable from a third party and a sum to amortise depreciating capital assets. The requirement to break even mentioned above must be examined carefully, for break even will mean different things in different circumstances, from, for example, not actually losing money to yielding enough to begin to repay debts but not enough to give the owner a spendable income.

Choice and the public

There may or there may not be on any estate, an opportunity to develop new activities, but meanwhile the processes of ownership continue bringing with them the need to make continual choices which in one year may be few and in another many. Tenants age and leave. Land falls vacant and must be occupied, but by whom? The owner knows that a largely un-informed public watches his actions and comments upon them, sometimes even offering advice. Part of the population wants to see the countryside "traditionally" farmed, whatever that may mean in terms of profit and production: part is not sure that any open land should be used for commercial purposes. Many people have been encouraged to like hardwoods and to dislike softwoods; to love beech and oak and to hate the "dark" conifer; to dislike change generally. The majority of landowners run their woodlands at a loss and in running them at all are often faced with public disapproval: disapproval of felling (the rape of the countryside); disapproval of planting (blocking the view or encouraging those "horrible" conifers): disapproval of thinning (destroying the young trees for profit and spoiling the woods). Almost everything the owner does in that part of his woodlands generally visible causes comment, most of it adverse: but if he does nothing few notice. Perhaps to gain public approval (should he want it) and to ease the strain on his purse he should neglect his woods? One must, however, appreciate that even woodland which is managed may appear from time to time to the public – and ashamedly occasionally to some part of urban officialdom – to be unmanaged. It is probably not often that the untutored public tries to tell, say a motor manufacturer, how to run his business, but few will fail to comment on farming or forestry when they see it.

Holistic management

Economic management may not be full management especially if it has an essentially short-term view. What is correctly done today may be approved today, but the long-term view of a problem, or even the long-term recognition of a problem, may produce a different or modified answer. Landownership is essentially the ownership of assets which develop and change over the years, linked as they are to growth, or perhaps just movement, in a changing environment – natural, economic, political and indeed moral. The linked businesses of ownership and occupation are dependent on each other and in the process of development and growth (and perhaps also of decline and shrinkage) affect people as well as properties and "things".

Economic land management must be holistic management; "holism" being defined as "a tendency in nature to form wholes which are more than the sum of the parts, by creative evolution". This surely is what management is trying to achieve, namely an organisation – the estate – which is indeed a whole being more than the sum of its parts. To attain this whole is to recognise the parts of which it is made up and from which it evolves so that the manager, the owner, must accept that the estate is not simply a collection of different landholdings differently operated for different purposes, but that it is also a collection of very different people some of whom are indeed using the land for business purposes but others as a basis of their life, a home. Holistic management should, therefore, treat each of the parts as contributing to the whole and not forget that people, as well as things, make up the whole.

The treatment of people as individuals with attributes, abilities, anxieties and hopes is as much land management as is the assessment of the financial returns immediately available. One does not give in to rogues, but an understanding of the personal impact of economic decisions made by an owner (or agent) is essential to the proper (holistic) development of the estate. A failing farm tenant may respond to a new opportunity offered or to the chance to give up with dignity and retire in the area in which he has made his life. This is holistic management. How far it is practised is a matter for debate. Whether it is more easily practised in the private sphere than in the public sphere is also a question with many answers. Who can more easily bend, or indeed break, the rules?

One can speculate and provide against speculation, but the land remains. Ownership is divisible and providing that successive generations serve the land as well or better than their forebears it matters little who is nominally in control. This of course is the crux of the whole matter. Are the land and those who live by it better cared for where ownership is maintained from generation to generation without disturbance or are tradition and an inherited love of the land mere figments of the imagination?

CHAPTER 7

The realisation of estate assets
– other land uses

Synopsis
Yields from property – Reasons for disposal – Imbalance between income and expenditure – Sales of land – Need for capital – Sale of estate assets – Surplus properties, houses and cottages – Redundant farm buildings – Tax implications – Development for non-agricultural uses – New land uses by tenants – Possible complications – Extraction of minerals – Tax consequences.

Introduction

It is well known that the average return on capital invested in the ownership of agricultural land which is let has, for at least 120 years been somewhere between 1% and 2% per annum, this being the yield after allowing for the deduction from the gross rents of all annual outgoings which the lessor has to meet out of those rents. There have been fluctuations in this yield from time to time when land values, but not rents, have dropped, a phenomenon which does not last long. Individual let farms may, of course, yield more or less than this; individual cottages and houses, accommodation lands, market gardens, gravel pits and the like variety of property will probably, though not always, produce a higher return.

Yields and disposals

Looked at as a single investment, the yield from let properties on a particular estate will depend upon the mix of those properties, but it is still unlikely to be above the yield on good class equity stocks and may well be below it. A low yield indicates a secure investment in the normal course of events, but a nil yield can indicate that there is no income: of course the yield to redemption (and when is that?) could well be different. In the context of the present chapter, redemption may be what it is all about. However, this chapter is not the place to discuss reasons for the different yields derived from different types of property (a particularly difficult exercise in relation to the variety of property types on the average agricultural estate); it must suffice to say that the generally low yield derived from the letting of farms places before the landowner the perhaps tempting possibility that the sale proceeds from a disposal of the whole estate, if wisely invested, will bring to him an income considerably greater than that which he presently enjoys, allied perhaps, but not certainly, to less security for the reinvested capital. This, coupled with the realisation that not to own and administer an agricultural estate and not to live in a large and draughty mansion house with little or no help will probably give rise to a quieter and more prosperous life, makes it tempting to wonder why agricultural landownership exists at all. Again, it is not the place of this book to attempt to answer that question except to point out that tradition maintained, a sense of responsibility for others, sporting opportunity, a certain social position and the opportunity to face and perhaps to solve difficulties and to wield power (which is attractive to some) and must jointly and severally have a bearing on the determination of many landowners to maintain their ownership. However, this chapter is not concerned with the temptations to dispose of the whole but with disposals of portions of the estate, with opportunities for disinvestment in landed property and with opportunities for non-agricultural development and use which may present themselves.

Expenditure and income

As a managed investment, land (in the legal sense) carries a permanent imbalance between income and expenditure, in that most of the income from agricultural rents is received only twice a year whereas the costs of management and of upkeep have to be met throughout the year on an almost daily basis; furthermore, sudden calls for expenditure on unplanned maintenance will occur from time to time – for example following a gale – which cannot be financially anticipated. Because of this imbalance between income and expenditure landed estates need a back-up of what has been called consociate capital – investments for example – which will yield an income which comes in at dates different from those on which rents are normally received and which can be called upon to provide easily accessible money to meet emergencies. Income from consociate capital helps to fill the gap between rent receipts: its ready availability precludes the wearisome and long drawn-out process involved in the sale of real property.

The need for capital

Where there is no outside capital to support the landed estate, or where there is not enough or where there is clearly idle capital in underused or unwanted real property or where, as is sometimes the case, such property is actually yielding a negative return (is in other words making an ownership loss because outgoings exceed income), it makes sense for the owner to sell and to put the proceeds to productive use. Many estates, perhaps indeed most of them, are supported by loans either by way of, hopefully, short-term overdrafts from the bank, which do fluctuate, or by way of specially arranged borrowings. The interest on these loans will not necessarily be relievable against taxable income and that must not be forgotten. In some cases, on the other hand, borrowings are self-financing (eg loans from the Agricultural Mortgage Corporation) and in other cases they are not.

Quite apart from the difficulties over the timing of the income flow and the need to be able to meet the annual costs of management and maintenance, there looms always over the estate the need to be able to replace, from time to time, worn-out buildings which have come to the end of their physical life (perhaps after very many years) or, more likely, of their economic life. In theory, of course, estate income from rents should, over the years, have been sufficient to provide for the replacement of worn-out fixed equipment, but in practice very few, if any, estates accumulate a building replacement sinking fund out of rents; income tax alone precludes this as a practical proposition. The need for external capital is, therefore, perpetual, namely to build up a consociate fund for additional income, to provide capital to meet emergencies and to provide, year by year, for replacements.

To sum up then, there are at least four reasons for the disposal of surplus lands (to which number may be added a fifth cynical one which is as valid as the rest), surplus lands being defined as those properties which are of little or no use to the estate. They can, of course, only be disposed of when there is a market for them.

1. To put the capital released by the disposal to some productive use (even if it is apparently no more immediately productive than the redemption of borrowings).
2. To build up a fund of consociate capital to augment estate income and to provide an easily realisable pool of funds to meet emergencies and to pay for renewals and reinvestments in the property.
3. To eliminate an estate property investment currently showing a negative return and which has little prospect of ever doing anything else.
4. To fund new initiatives.
5. To meet the owner's need or desire for a new plaything.

No doubt some of these reasons overlap in that they may be expressed more simply as the need to put certain estate resources to better and/or more profitable use.

Sale of assets

The process of selling various estate assets has been going on for a long time. The changes in farming practice over the last 30 years or so have, by and large, produced bigger units, an increase in the number and size of machinery and a reduction in the labour force. This, on many estates, with similar changes in forestry practice, has resulted in a reduction in the number of cottages which are needed for estate and farm employees and a reduction in the number and type of farm buildings required, partly because farming systems have changed and partly because many buildings are unsuitable for modern use having been designed for different purposes.

Surplus cottages are relatively easy to sell in the right area, although not all owners and not all farmers want to find strangers owning and living in cottages and houses in the centre of the estate or farm. They can be disruptive and a nuisance. On sale a house's use as a dwelling will not change and, therefore, unless it is presently subject to a planning requirement that it be occupied only by persons engaged in agriculture, no new planning consents are required before it can be put on the market. The fact that a house may be suitable for (or need) improvement or enlargement does not detract from its value to a prospective country-dweller: indeed, sometimes the prospect of gentrification is positively attractive.

Redundant buildings

The amalgamation of farms has led to farmsteads, or parts of them, becoming redundant, including not only buildings but also substantial farmhouses. The houses can almost always be sold (if they must be) or let on short or long leases, but what to do with the buildings is often a problem. To leave them to fall into ruin does not seem to be good estate management (though it could be good financial management); to sell them to the first bidder may be called careless. Thought and planning is necessary. In many cases conversion and letting for office, light industrial or craft use has been successful. In these sort of cases the estate retains the freehold ownership, the tenants taking longer or shorter leases, with the responsibility for financing the conversion or for fitting out for the particular use proposed. Circumstances and opportunities alter cases and whether the estate does the conversion and then lets, or indeed sells, the resulting unit or whether the lessees do so is a matter for decision in the light of the time, the place and the opportunity. In other cases conversion of redundant farmbuildings for office use or for dwellings in "courtyard developments" may appear to provide a solution. To dispose of the freehold of a set of buildings, for whatever purpose, situated in the middle of the estate or farm could well be to lose that control often essential to ensure the continuing well-being of all concerned. Residential development in particular can give rise to conflict between users whether they are tenants or freeholders. In all these cases certain salient points need to be addressed, namely:

1. The problem of obtaining the necessary consent from the planning authority for the use proposed. This is a complex subject and one which often needs a tactical approach. How to facilitate the getting of planning consent is not a subject for discussion here, but co-operation, consultation and persuasion often bring faster results than confrontation.

2. The need to "sell" the proposals to the local inhabitants, who often object, almost in principle. Fierce objection to change is a characteristic of both the old and the new inhabitant.

3. A need to retain some control over future use (as mentioned above).

4. A reasonable certainty that the changes proposed do not adversely affect the proper use of the adjacent lands.

It is necessary to consider the taxation implications of the leases or sales proposed. Disposals will give rise to a potential charge to capital gains tax and rollover relief may not be available; leases for 50 years or less, demanding premiums or requiring lessees to carry out improvements, will give rise to special charges under Schedule A or Schedule D, the premiums or other sums being treated as part taxable income and part capital gain. (Taxes Act 1988 section 34 *et seq*). Indeed, gains on disposals may be charged to income tax and not capital gains tax if the transactions are caught under Taxes Act 1988 section 776. New non-agricultural uses of lands and buildings previously used for agriculture may eliminate inheritance tax reliefs on agricultural land, farmbuildings and houses.

Development for non-agricultural use

Land uses change; some prosper, some decline. It is difficult, perhaps impossible, to envisage so extensive a decline in the major use of rural land, that of farming, that it becomes a minor land use. Nevertheless, the future of farming today is uncertain and it struggles, in some areas at least, against hardships which have been largely unknown since the 1940s, and both the agricultural landowner and occupier need to search out new ventures by the use of which they may provide against an uncertain future. Some areas of the country have been harder hit by adversity than others, particularly the uplands of the North and West.

It has been suggested by Professor Newby in his Royal Agricultural Society of England Annual Lecture 1993 that farms in different areas should be set different objectives, some for food production, some to sustain the social fabric of remote rural communities, some to maintain a rural environment attractive to the nation at large and for which it has indicated a willingness to pay. All areas, whatever their objective under the present or under a new policy, can benefit from an inflow of income derived from the diversification of businesses within the rural sphere and from the introduction of successful new ventures. Farm tenants may find new non-agricultural uses for their land and buildings. Landowners may do the same and may, to maintain or increase their rents, encourage their tenants to adopt new enterprises (providing those tenants have the skills and knowledge to run them). At this point the economics and initiative of land management must step in.

The position of the tenant

Some landowners insist that their tenants must farm as they have contracted to do and that any use of land or buildings which does not conform to the agricultural use for which the tenancy agreement provides cannot be permitted, or may only be allowed following a re-negotiation of the tenancy. There are as yet no rules about such a situation, no practice notes to follow and each case on each estate must be treated on its merits, relying not only on the law but also on an assessment of the proposing tenant and on the general attitude of the owner: there are, however, points within the sphere of land law and the law of taxation which must be considered when coming to a decision about how to deal with non-agricultural uses from the point of view of landlord and tenant.

Landlords and tenants

At the time when this chapter was written no drastic changes had been made to the law of agricultural holdings as introduced originally by the Agricultural Holdings Act 1948 and as continued by the 1986 Act, but during the following months the Agricultural Tenancies Bill has been going through Parliament. This will, if enacted, make possible the creation of the Farm Business Tenancy under the provisions of which a landlord and tenant of an agricultural holding will, in a new letting, be able to agree to the use of part of an agricultural holding for non-agricultural purposes. However, these provisions will not affect tenancies in existence when the Bill became law so that what follows is valid as far as these lettings are concerned.

1. Where any planning consent is obtained, either specifically or by means of "deemed consent" for the use of land or buildings for a purpose other than agriculture, then the landlord can give his tenant a valid notice to quit that part of the holding, to which the tenant cannot object.

2. A landlord who accepts rent from his tenant following a breach by the tenant of any of the terms of his agreement of which he is aware (or should be) has condoned the breach, though if the breach is a continuing one he can, on a subsequent occasion, refuse the rent and will thereon cease to condone the breach. Thus, a landlord whose farming tenant proceeds to use part of his holding

for a non-agricultural purpose could put himself in the wrong by accepting rent and thus condoning the breach, leaving himself in a difficult position should he subsequently wish to re-negotiate the tenancy.

3. The agricultural letting is subject to the Agricultural Holdings legislation and to the protection afforded by it. A business letting is subject to the Landlord and Tenant Act 1954 and to the protection afforded by it, but where the business is partly agricultural and partly something else then if the agricultural use is substantial the whole letting will be under the Agricultural Holdings legislation; the general rule being that where there is a change of use from, say agricultural to other business use (or the other way round), the protection given to the original use will subsist unless the new use becomes the dominant one. The use of a minor part of an agricultural holding for a non-agricultural purpose will leave the letting protected by the Agricultural Holdings legislation.

The landlord asked by his tenant to consent to a non-agricultural business use of part of the holding could refuse consent outright, give consent outright (re-negotiating the terms or not) or be willing to consider the proposal if the tenant surrenders that part of the holding and takes a new letting of it as a business tenancy under the Landlord and Tenant Act 1954. In such a case it is possible for landlord and tenant by mutual agreement to approach the court with a request that the tenancy be not subject to those parts of the 1954 Act which provide for automatic renewal of the tenancy when it comes to an end.

Valuation relief applicable to the agricultural value (where the transferor qualifies) on the transfer of agricultural property may be put in jeopardy by a non-agricultural use. If the non-agricultural business part of the holding is let separately there can be no agricultural valuation relief on that part: if the business use is co-incident with the agricultural use and there is no separate letting if that use increases the value of the holding above its agricultural value, then clearly the excess value should get no agricultural relief; but whether, or when, the use of a small part of the holding for non-agricultural purposes will cause that part to be separated out (as in law it certainly could be) is uncertain. Business property relief itself would not be available unless the property was "relevant business property", the business were being run by the transferor, and he qualified for the relief.

As suggested earlier, a landlord may welcome the initiative of a farming tenant who diversifies his farming business to bring in additional income, whether that be agricultural or not, for it provides the landlord with additional security for the rent and, indeed, may provide additional rent itself. However, the landlord may properly feel that he should reassess the whole letting if the tenant is allowed to profit from the use of land let to him for one purpose now partly superseded. Often a non-agricultural use involves the adaptation or conversion of buildings: if such is to happen who is to pay for it and upon what conditions? Will the conversion be permanent or temporary, easily rectified on a reletting or not? Is there room for a negotiated settlement? Should the landowner share the cost, meet the whole or let the tenant do the work and what about compensation due to the tenant on his quitting the holding? These are questions, not answers.

Mineral extraction

The working of land for the extraction of minerals is hardly a diversification of the land from its prime use for agriculture, for such extraction is to an extent the using up of part of the land itself and is not merely an alternative use which can be abandoned for the original use at will. It is, indeed, a part disposal of the land (and is to a degree treated as such for taxation purposes). Proposals to use land for mineral extraction will often meet with vociferous local objection because of the fears that the side-effects will have a traumatic effect on the local countryside by way, for example, of a permanent change in the landscape and considerable disruption during the process of extraction and transportation. Not all minerals are in the ownership of the person who owns the land in which they lie; gold, silver and precious metals are vested in the Crown for example, but other minerals, notably stone, sand and gravel, may be exploited by the owner of the land in different ways, namely by extracting them himself (as sole trader, partner or through the agency of a company) or by allowing somebody else to do so. The matter of running a minerals extraction business is not for consideration here, but a few points appropriate to the exploitation of land for mineral extraction by third parties are perhaps worth thought.

A simple and clean-cut way of realising the value of minerals which lie under land is to sell the land containing them. This gives rise to few taxation problems. The profit will be subject to tax on the capital gain which will depend upon the base value of the land on acquisition or on March 31 1982, the amount of the indexation allowance available and the price or value for which the sale is made. It is, on the other hand, possible to sell the subsurface minerals while retaining the freehold of the surface. In both these cases the operator-purchaser will certainly not pay the full market value of the minerals at the date of the sale, for he will need to allow for the fact that he will only be able to realise the minerals over a length of time. Following a sale if he was using the land for his business the vendor will be able to claim rollover relief if he reinvests the proceeds in the same or another business.

Instead of a sale the owner will often prefer to grant a mineral lease, partly to ensure that he gets full value over time for the minerals to be extracted, partly to retain some control over the operations and partly to have complete control over what is left after the lease has come to an end. The normal arrangement is for the owner to lease the land for extraction and to charge a royalty on the amount of minerals extracted each year. There may in addition to this be a fixed rent reserved, say, for access to the site. Such a rent is charged to income tax under Schedule A in the normal way; the royalty payment, however, is treated specially in that it is, in the first instance, subject to deduction of basic rate tax at source by the payee. From the recipient's point of view the royalty each year is treated each year half as income assessed under Schedule D (from which half the owner's management expenses in connection with the minerals lease may be deducted) and half as a chargeable capital gain (from which no deductions are allowed). The income tax deducted at source by the lessee satisfies the lessor's liability to basic rate tax on both the income portion and on the chargeable gain. The only relief available to the landowner is given when the lease comes to an end for then (if he should dispose of what is left) he may be able to establish a capital gains tax loss or he may opt for a deemed disposal so that a terminal loss may be established. In either case the loss arising may be carried back and set off against the capital gains element of the royalties over the preceding 15 years or it may at his option be carried forward to set against future chargeable gains. There is of course no certainty that any terminal loss will arise, for that will depend upon the base value of the land at the date of acquisition and the value of that now held, which may be restored land or perhaps a large hole in the ground or lake with valuable potential use.

When considering the exploitation of minerals it is worth bearing in mind three special points. First, if a sale is made subject to the vendor's right to repurchase at the end of the extraction period the difference between the sale price and repurchase price may be taxed and treated as a premium under a lease for 50 years or less (part income and part capital gain). Second, agricultural property relief for inheritance tax purposes will be lost on the extraction site and business property relief only gained if the owner is running the minerals business. Third, the existence of known mineral reserves on farmland may bring the value above the agricultural value so that no agricultural property relief will be available on the excess, though, if the land is being farmed by the owner, business property relief may be available on the value in excess of the agricultural value.

In any arrangement for selling or letting care must be taken to ensure that the site is properly fenced at all times, that access roads and tracks are surely defined together with their use and that precise conditions are laid down for reinstatement of the land worked both during the works and after their completion. Where land is let for stone quarrying it is often possible and usually desirable to restrict the times when rock-blasting may take place.

CHAPTER 8

Farm tenancies

Synopsis

Landlords felt left out of upturn in farming fortunes after war – Perceived fiscal and legal disadvantages. Agricultural Holdings Act 1986 offers some redress but landlords remain hesitant to let – Survival of present system in some cases – Need for an alternative to meet changed circumstances – Future.

The decline

The history of the farm tenancy system since the Second World War has been one of continued contraction. Landlords have been increasingly disinclined to commit themselves to what they have seen as an arrangement financially and fiscally at a disadvantage compared to keeping land in hand and, thus, available for disposal with vacant possession. Deep down, however, it has been the legal inflexibility combined with the political threat that has been a decisive influence.

1 Profitability compared

After the war, most landed estates found themselves with a number of let farms, which appeared to form a very unattractive investment. With the increase in tractor power and mechanisation and the trend to machine milking, considerable capital investment was needed. However, many let farms were small in size and recent legislation had prevented the owner from obtaining vacant possession without the tenant's consent, so that he could not easily amalgamate uneconomically small holdings, relet them and spread the necessary capital required over a larger acreage. In addition, a considerable backlog of repairs had built up during the depression of the 1930s, when rents were low (and often in arrears) and this had been accentuated by six years of war and building controls, the latter enduring until 1951.

While logically the delayed repairs might have been financed out of increased rents, the landlord found this avenue for fund raising virtually closed by a freeze on rents until 1947 when the Agriculture Act of that year ushered in a decade of farm rent control, which effectively prevented the landlord from sharing in the profitability of farming and accumulating the reserves of money from which the improvements and repairs might have been met. It is not difficult to see why owners felt that agricultural prosperity had passed them by and why many of them sold their estates, giving their tenants the opportunity to buy the freehold on the equity of the land. Nor is it difficult to see why many estates seized the opportunity when a farm became vacant, to take it in hand and regain the flexibility of tenure which legislation had denied them as landlords.

Indeed, until the Agriculture Act 1958 landowners saw themselves as left out of the profitable business their tenant farmers appeared to be enjoying. Even after that Act had sought to redress this imbalance, valuers were still disinclined to implement its literal meaning and rents did not rise up to expectations. The fact that many landowners had not the liquid resources to enter farming and when they did so, had neither the expertise nor the will to profit by it was often overlooked. When land became vacant it was seldom relet. The home farm became larger and the patchwork of tenanted holdings on the estate, so familiar on estate maps of the 1950s, disappeared.

2 The fiscal disadvantages

Even if the landowner felt the profits of farming insufficiently alluring, he would still find it hard to ignore what he heard about the tax advantages of owner-occupation. Traditionally tax laws have favoured the trader in ways not always shared by the landlord. The farmer can claim relief against taxable income for his machinery and any losses he may suffer. Indeed, stories abounded of farmers who purchased run-down properties, renovated them on their farming account and resold at a substantial profit. The restrictions placed on tax reliefs for hobby farming losses in 1960 and the introduction of capital gains tax in 1965 were intended, among other things, to remedy such abuses, but the opportunities still appeared to be there for the well-advised.

The fact that the landlord could also set revenue losses on his tenanted farms against other income indefinitely was not usually appreciated. Moreover, the opportunity presented to him by the one-estate election, where the upkeep of his house and of in-hand properties could be offset against his rents, again indefinitely, was sometimes overlooked or felt to be an inadequate recompense for what he had lost.

Whatever the true legal and fiscal position of the agricultural landlord, he and his advisers convinced themselves that farm tenancies were not the best way forward for the landed estate and have consistently been looking for other ways to maintain estate income from the land. To make matters worse, the incoming government in 1974 announced the introduction of a capital transfer tax with no hint of a concession to owners of let land. Over the years reliefs have in fact been extended to agricultural landlords, but the damage had been done. About the same time, a Green Paper on a wealth tax was tabled and this too paid scant recognition to the low income that could be generated from let land from which the tax would have to be paid. The Labour Party manifesto of 1979 read "In the next Parliament, we shall introduce an annual Wealth Tax on those whose total net personal wealth exceeds £150,000 . . .". The general proposition was that the tax would start at 1%, rising to 5% on assets exceeding £5m. So a landowner with 150 acres of let land would probably enter the wealth tax net while the possession of 5,000 acres would attract the top rate. It has been argued that with the return of a Conservative government in 1979, the quantity of land let should have risen. Unfortunately, the position was not so simple. Memories lingered and the likelihood of a change of government in 1983, 1987 and again in 1992 were not conducive to a lifetime commitment to the tenanted system.

3 The legal framework

On the legal side the story has been one of continued well-intentioned efforts to protect the farm tenant from eviction either from notice to quit or from a rent that left him with no alternative but to leave. These efforts have succeeded in protecting existing tenants almost completely, but excluded many would-be entrants to farming along the tenanted route, for it was virtually closed. In 1950 62% of the farming acreage in the UK was tenanted; by 1990 it had fallen to 39%. Even these figures conceal a number of family tenancies where the land is in hand in all but name.

Until the war, the basis of farm rents was supply and demand. There was no legal limit to the rent a landlord could ask. In the 1930s, a time of depression, landlords were principally worried lest they had unoccupied land and no rental income – a scenario hardly known to present-day farmers, landlords and agents!

4 Arbitrators' interpretation of "rent properly payable"

In the Agriculture Act 1947, confirmed in the Agricultural Holdings Act 1948, section 24, security of tenure for life was given to farm tenants. Under section 8 a procedure was laid down for referring the rent to arbitration, but beyond enjoining the arbitrator to ignore tenants' improvements and to ignore grant-aided works carried out by the landlord, no other basis for the rent was given other than that it should be the "rent properly payable". Arbitrations were few, but generally arbitrators, whether appointed by mutual agreement or failing agreement, by the Minister of Agriculture, tended to ignore scarcity and open tender rents. They took a conservative view of what the tenant could pay so that rents had risen from about £1.50 per acre in 1948 to about £2.00 by 1958, although in real terms they had dropped to about £1.33! Some of the reasons for this lay in the inevitable results that come from restricting market forces. To the tenant, rent was the share of the surplus due to the owner after the tenant had taken his just reward for his enterprise and skill. The landlord, however, sought a return on capital after providing for the upkeep of the fixed equipment which was imposed on him by law. Carried to its logical conclusion, the tenant's view could reduce the net rent of a marginal farm to a minus figure after the landlord's obligations had been met.

Had the market been unfettered by legislation, rents should have found their market level, the price of land should have reflected these rents and the paradoxes which beset let land rents and values would not have existed – or would they? The answer will never be known because the open market was controlled by a security of tenure given to the tenant at a rent often determined by valuers who sought to be fair to the tenant at the landlord's expense. As a result, landowners saw themselves as left out of a share of the profitable business their tenant farmers appeared to be enjoying.

The Agriculture Act 1958 defined the rent properly payable as that at which "the holding might reasonably be expected to be let in the open market by a willing landlord to a willing tenant". In theory, rents might have been expected to escalate in line with the high tender rents that were offered on the rare occasions that land came available for letting. In practice, arbitrators remained very conservative on rents and were reluctant to use these tender rents without making considerable allowance for the premium they saw included in the figures.

5 Succession 1976

While the basis of rent had moved marginally in favour of the landlord, the inflexibility of let land as an investment remained, tied as it was to lifetime tenure. It was unfortunate, therefore, that in 1976 a measure was introduced into a non-controversial Agriculture Bill granting succession to two further generations of farm tenants. This shut the door on regaining possession for most landowners and their living heirs. It may be said that had there been any life left in the tenanted system in 1976, this measure effectively ended it.

The legal safeguards protecting the tenant could have been modified to make them more acceptable to the landlord. They could, moreover, have been more realistically interpreted, but they were not and rents remained low even after 1958. However, it was probably the political threat to landownership from 1945 until the late 1980s which ultimately weighed with landowners and influenced estate policy.

6 New definition of rent 1984

In 1984, as a result of discussions between the National Farmers Union and the Country Landowners Association, a "package" was agreed which was embodied in the Agricultural Holdings Act 1984 and subsequently formed section 12 of the Agricultural Holdings Act 1986. This reads:

The rent properly payable in respect of a holding shall be the rent at which the holding might reasonably be expected to be let by a prudent and willing landlord to a prudent and willing tenant, taking into account (subject to sub-paragraph (3) and paragraphs 2 and 3 below) all relevant factors, including (in every case) the terms of the tenancy (including those relating to rent), the character and situation of the holding (including the locality in which it is situated), *the productive capacity of the holding* and *comparable lettings* as determined in accordance with sub-paragraph (3) below . . .

The new definition omitted reference to the "open market" to try to eliminate the premium of tender rents. It also introduced for the first time a reference to "the productive capacity of the holding". Interestingly, valuers had often resorted to farm budgets to justify their rental figures, splitting the surplus between landlord and tenant and this now received a semblance of statutory approval. Two finely balanced factors now came to determine "the rent properly payable"; one being productive capacity, which since 1989 has tended to have a constraining influence on the rent, while the other, comparable lettings, often reflecting tender rents and the better days of the 1980s, helped to maintain rent levels at figures increasingly difficult to justify on productivity alone.

7 The political background

The nationalisation of land was not on the political agenda of the Labour Government in the 1940s, nor was it when it was elected in 1964. Nevertheless, it was thought to be on a hidden agenda by those who had most to lose by such a measure. When, therefore, the White Paper *The Land Commission* was published in September 1965, with the avowed intention of taxing development gains, many landowners saw it as the precursor of a vehicle for the expropriation of private land. The fact that the measure stopped short at its original intention did not entirely remove these suspicions. In 1974, when Labour returned to power, an influential group headed by Professor Nicholas Kaldor[1] put forward an ingenious scheme for taking over all land over 99 years which would have been inexpensive and relatively simple. In the end it did not come to fruition but *Farmland Market*[2] commenting at the time on the nationalisation of land needed for development wrote,

But though the official line is now no more than the public ownership of land for development, it should not be assumed that Labour does not intend to move further. Many Labour MPs favour full-blooded land nationalisation and can be expected to push hard for it if the party gets back to power after the next election with a really workable majority.

In the end this threat was limited to a plan in the Labour manifesto of 1979 whereby tenanted land only would be taken over by the local authority. At an agricultural conference at Cambridge in 1981 Gavin Strang, Labour's front bench spokesman on agriculture, affirmed that to arrest the decline in opportunities for new entrants

1 *The case for nationalising* (1974) Campaign for nationalising land, 139 Old Church Street, London SW3 6EB.
2 "Land Values 1974" *Farmland Market* August 1974, Estates Gazette.

and "to ensure that a large acreage of our land is developed and maintained as a national asset there is no alternative to public ownership"[1]. The overlying political threat to land, and specifically tenanted land, ensured that confidence in the tenanted sector for the private landowner has not returned. If two events were to be selected for their influence on landowning opinion, they would be the extension of succession in the Agriculture Act 1976 and the threat to nationalise let land. Fiscal, legal and profitability factors played their part, in no small degree governed by political theory, but the underlying hostility of some sections of the electorate, and those they elect, to the agricultural landlord has driven the latter to become an owner-occupier in which role he stands alongside the small proprietors of Wales and other areas with whom the most radical left would hesitate to seek confrontation.

Where now?

1 A new initiative

The Agricultural Tenancies Act of 1995 was the outcome of a new initiative based on a consensus arrived at in 1993 by the Country Landowners Association, the National Farmers' Union, the Royal Institution of Chartered Surveyors, the Tenant Farmers Association and the National Federation of Young Farmers Clubs. It went almost the whole way to meet all those objections dealt with in the earlier part of this chapter and which have dissuaded landowners from letting their farms. It allowed the parties to fix the rent and agree contractual terms on the frequency and any specific increases of rent during the term of the tenancy. It allowed the tenant to diversify into other businesses without the risk that such businesses might put the tenancy at risk or bring it under the Landlord and Tenant Act 1954 to the landlord's disadvantage. It ensured that the landlord could recover vacant possession of the farm on the termination of the lease or in the case of annual tenancies, on the giving of the necessary notice. The shadow Labour opposition confirmed that the party, if returned to power, would not seek to reverse these arrangements retrospectively. When the Government extended 100% inheritance tax relief to *new* lettings made after September 1 1995 (when the new Act came into force) and the opposition

---

1 Savills Agricultural Conference, December 17 1981, Churchill College, Cambridge.

confirmed its policy to equate capital tax for let and in-hand land, the omens could not have appeared more favourable for a return to the tenanted system.

2 Lingering doubts about the new legislation

While so much has been done to restore the confidence of landowners in the letting of their farms, there remain lingering doubts on both sides. To understand this, it is important to bear in mind some of the essential differences between the occupation of a farm by a farmer and his family and that of business premises by a small trader. The farmer makes the farm his home. It is likely that his wife and in due course his children will become involved in the practical working of the business and in its management decisions. Living as they do "over the shop" they are emotionally involved in the property in a way less often encountered in other fields of commerce. This leads to problems if they are asked to move, which in turn leads to fewer farms becoming available. Thus, the family asked to quit a farm suffers not only the emotional upset of leaving its roots but the added problem of having, since 1945, nowhere else to move to. In the same way, but to a lesser extent, the landowner living on his estate as most private landowners do, seeks something more from his property than the owners of business premises or more recently the owner of an out-of-town trading estate. Not only does he often live surrounded by his farms but he and his family regularly meet his farming tenants socially, in the village. In addition, he may shoot or ride over their land and extract his timber across their fields. He undertakes to maintain those farmers' houses and buildings. This intimate connection with the tenants has had a healthy social effect and has humanised an otherwise business arrangement. Nevertheless, it has contained a source of friction and has provided more opportunities for conflict of interest than exists in the ownership of other business property. The smaller the landed estate becomes, the more the constraints on his freedom to do what he likes with his own will irritate the owner and so circumstances build up which make the system unsuitable for him.

So it is that among those who would be tenants there are those opposed to the application of the open market to a system that has, for so many years, been shielded from it. The new Act has been criticised as a return to the law of the jungle. The spectre of young tenants moving into farms under new revised free-market tenancy legislation, highly vulnerable to capricious landlords may however be a false one. Young people setting out on the great adventure of farming are unlikely to place their tenant's capital in a conventional landlord's farm complete with farmhouse, buildings and land. They are unlikely to win the support of their bank or any other backers if they have no security of tenure and they are highly unlikely, as has been pointed out above, to find a landlord prepared to place himself in the invidious position of having to make such tenants farmless and homeless should he need possession.

At the same time there remain landowners whose circumstances would suggest that a tenancy of their farmland would be in their best interests but who draw back from a step they see as irrevocable. Their reservation is based on a knowledge that no political commitment is sacrosanct and that they may live to regret the granting of a tenancy when there remain systems of occupation which may still have much to commend them. The medium sized and smaller estates are most likely to be reluctant to let land which, should it become alienated, might damage the estate as a proprietary unit particularly if such land adjoins the principal house or contains valuable minerals beneath the surface. There will also be owners whose future estate policy is not settled and who cannot afford to sign away any option that may be needed in the future.

3 Continuing demand for a tenanted system

There remains, however, a demand for the longer term farm tenancy with some security for the tenant, a degree of flexibility as to the terms each party may impose on the other and a relatively 'safe' rental income to the landowner. There will be owners whose circumstances or personal preferences do not envisage taking land in hand or enlarging the home farm if such exists. For them the new legislation will help perpetuate their policy of letting their land and may indeed tip the scales in favour of letting farms that fall vacant. There will be owners who are content to commit their land in this way and will feel that any political risk and the greatly lessened legal and fiscal constraints are compensated by a reduced capital and management commitment.

These owners will also include the traditional institutions such as the Church, the Crown and the older universities. Debarred or inhibited by their charitable status from active farming, they are, however, deeply invested in land and unlikely to be affected by any confiscatory legislation. At the same time, being able to take a very long-term view of their investment, they can bide their time until development or vacant possession through death comes their way when the opportunity will be there to profit from the years of waiting. In most respects they are ideally situated for the traditional tenanted market and the history of their investments clearly gives them the confidence to remain in land. To these must be added the National Trust with over 400,000 acres of land. While unable to sell much of its land, even if it chose to, it provides a solid core of let land for the foreseeable future.

The newer institutions have a much shorter history of investment in land. The Northfield Report was commissioned by a government which responded to fears that gradually most land, certainly let land, would be owned by financial institutions and this was felt to be socially unacceptable. This report showed that only 1.2% was so owned and much of the concern arose from the fact that with only 2% of land coming on the market each year, the relatively minuscule areas purchased by the institutions appeared a more serious matter than it really was. In the end many of these companies have sold their landed investment and appear reluctant to re-enter this market. Were they to do so, it is hard to see how else they would arrange for the land to be occupied and farmed other than through a farm tenancy.

The same may be said of local authority land. During the first half of this century county councils were encouraged to purchase land and provide smallholdings to give younger farmers a first step on the farming ladder. It met a popular conception that society should encourage a return to the land. While many of these farms are still in existence, they are being run down. Not only have local authorities and their tax-paying electors found just how expensive it is to own tenanted land but it has been questioned how far one small section of society should so be assisted.

There is still a sizeable number of owners who have sufficient available land to feel relaxed with a tenanted system where the loss of such land, if it occurred, would not pose a threat to the core of the estate and they will continue to treat such land as an investment and to let it. Hesitation may exist where demand is foreseen for heavy capital expenditure on, for instance, the house or even to meet capital taxes. Ironically, in the latter case owners will be tempted to keep possession of the land to secure the maximum tax relief.

4 New role for the larger estate

There may be the opportunity for larger landowners to provide estate farm services for their tenants as well as for the home farm. Ministry of Agriculture grant aid since the war has not really catered for the setting up of such installations as co-operative corn stores, fertiliser stores or communal processing buildings. This was not so in France nor indeed in Yugoslavia where the Serb peasant farmers, who retained ownership of their land under Tito, formed state-run co-operative stores and processing plants where the purchase and sale of produce was handled by well-paid operatives usually of high quality.

Could the farm manager, bereft of some of his day-to-day worries by the use of machinery syndicates, fill a role here? It would require the removal of two obstacles:

1. The individualism of farmers who have preferred to do their own thing and who often have sons and labour available. The part-time tenant farmer might, however, be far more inclined to be relieved of trying to be a mechanic, agronomist and marketeer all rolled into one!

2. The ability of the estate to "collectivise" their tenants, retain their confidence and convince them that it was not merely an attempt by the home farm to spread its overheads.

It is likely that only very large estates could help perform this role and the opportunity has probably been lost if it ever existed.

5 The alternatives for the future

A high proportion of land available for renting, which owners are prepared to make available for tenancies being, as stated above, land unlikely to pose a threat to the estate should it be alienated for any reason, will be let to larger adjoining farmers, who will be seeking to expand their acreage for a variety of reasons. They may wish to replace their set-aside acres or they may merely wish to spread their overheads over an increasingly larger acreage to compete with the market. They are unlikely to be farmers who will be dependent on the landlord for their home or, indeed, for the main core of their livelihood.

Indeed, these farmers, by virtue of the equipment which they possess, the quotas for livestock which they have recently secured and the expertise with which they have to deal with new market conditions, may be men and women highly in demand and eagerly sought after by landowners in circumstances that last prevailed in the 1930s. Such men, masters of their industry, are highly unlikely to put themselves in a position where they could be vulnerable to the whims of a landowner. At the other end of the spectrum, the smaller family farmer is likely to be one who is based on a small acreage which he owns or rents under existing "secure" legislation and he will likewise seek to expand by renting available land. Again, he is unlikely to take on let land for which he has not got the necessary equipment and he will, if he is wise, avoid placing himself in a vulnerable position.

A third group of farmers has already begun to emerge and these own or rent very little land indeed, but are mainly arable contractors, contract milkers or flock-masters. They may earn their livelihood entirely by their contract work or their skill with dairying, sheep or livestock. They may in time build up a relationship with one or more landowners in a way that gives them an opportunity to enter into an arrangement with those owners giving them a chance to share the profits by "contract farming", partnership or even a tenancy. In turn, they may thereby gain a greater stake in the land which they farm. This is, of course, a negation of all that agricultural holdings legislation has stood for over the years, but the fact must be faced that a very widespread need had been left unsatisfied by the previous system and a way had to be found for individual entrepreneurial aspirations in farming. The tenanted system is not dead. It has its part to play as shown earlier, but even in its new form may not be capable of serving all sections of the industry; it has not been so for some time.

CHAPTER 9

Farmland values

Synopsis
A study of factors inherent in property determining its value –
Residential – Agricultural productivity and land grade – Development
– Size of transaction – Sporting – Farmbuildings – Landscape.
Factors external to property – Purchaser motives – Spreading
overheads – Farm structure in the locality – Supply and demand –
Taxation. Future.

Introduction

In 1889, a time of agricultural depression, the estate agents Norton
Trist & Gilbert wrote a letter to the *Times* in which they quoted the
annual average price, rental value and number of years' purchase
(rate of return) of the land their firm had sold from 1781 to 1880[1].
They concluded with the view that

rent is not the full measure of the benefits of landholding, and that [land has]
fetched these large number of years' purchase . . . shows that the amenities
attached to land were much appreciated.

During the period they were reviewing, those amenities included
political influence and social prestige as well as the residential
premium and Norton Trist & Gilbert were probably hoping that all
these benefits would cushion the fall in capital values. In the event,
the price of farmland (which was then 90% tenanted) fell from £56
per acre in 1875 to £19 per acre in the 1890s, and remained below
£28 per acre, the level it had reached in the Napoleonic period,
even in the 1914–18 War. No doubt it would have fallen even further
but for the residual non-agricultural attractions which persisted into
the 20th century and which are now thought by some observers to

---

1 Peters, GH, Parsons, DT and Patchett, DM (1982) *A Century of Land Values*, in
Oxford Agrarian Studies vol II, The Institute of Agricultural Economics, Oxford.

have transformed the market out of all recognition. In the late 1980s land prices over 40 years have diverged from farm income significantly and the relationship of land prices to that of gross product price weakened as the table below shows.

Table 1 Land values by land grade – a phenomenon of the 1980s

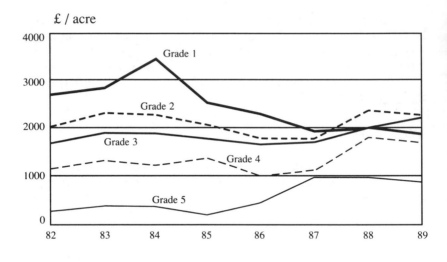

Source: MAFF/AMC CALP Series

The fact is that a "farm" is a complex bundle of assets comprising not just the potential for agricultural income but for other sources of income and personal satisfaction and enjoyment. This is why almost any farm may possess attraction to some buyer. It is this that makes any analysis of farmland price so difficult and any prediction of value so hazardous. While most estate agents refer to their sale results in terms of price per acre, and it is hard to see how else they can base their prices, it ignores the complexities which may account for over half the value. This chapter, therefore, tries to isolate and evaluate these component parts that contribute to farmland prices.

The residential factor

In 1989 Savills Research Department stated that "residential potential and housing quality now have a greater influence on land prices than land grades or enterprise type"[1]. Investors in land are bound to ask themselves whether, in the light of agriculture's current prospects, non-agricultural factors really are so important that they offset the effects of dwindling farm incomes. If not, then the investor could be saddled with a very long-term investment.

The data on which the above assessment of amenity value was based requires close scrutiny. Savills sell about one-seventh of the UK farmland acreage traded each year, more than any of their rivals. Table 2 shows how the total paid for 84 farms and blocks of land sold through Savills in 1991 can be split into "components of value". The components of each sale were valued by the selling agent and these figures are the totals for each component.

Table 2 Total value breakdown

Bare land	18,371,800
Houses	13,015,668
Farmbuildings	1,281,000
Woodland	988,270
Sporting	25,000
Development	826,000
Let land/buildings	707,000
Dairy quota	945,000
Total (approx)	36,159,738

Source: Savills

The table shows that house prices accounted for 36% of total value, which demonstrates how misleading "per acre" land prices can be when the price includes a house.

Another guide as to the proportion of farmland value represented by housing is to be found in Ministry of Agriculture, Fisheries and Food (MAAF) data. MAFF publishes yearly and six-monthly mean prices for land according to region, tenure, size of transaction and whether the sale included buildings. Taking vacant possession land,

---

1 Savills Research (1989) unpublished data.

which comprises about 90% of the UK acreage sold each year, and assuming that buildings accounted for the whole of the price differential between land with and without buildings, the estimated value for buildings sold with vacant possession farmland in the same regions as the Savills samples, for the same period, came to 20% of the value of all vacant possession sales. Assuming that the value of houses relative to farmbuildings was the same in the MAFF as in the Savills data, namely 10:1, this would mean that the housing component was worth 18% of the total sales. Bearing in mind, however, that the MAFF data included all land sales and less than 50% of these sales included a house, it is reasonable to ascribe a much higher proportion of the sale value to the house in the MAFF data where a house was included in the sale.

Table 3 Average price of vacant possession land with buildings, per hectare, by region (1991)

	South East	East Anglia	East Midlands	South West
MAFF	£6,845	£5,511	£3,868	£6,953
Savills	£10,966	£5,601	£4,344	£8,591

Average price of vacant possession land without buildings

MAFF	£4,141	£4,056	£3,519	£3,874
Savills	–	£3,740	£3,775	£4,059

A third source of information on the components of farmland values comes from some research in an unpublished thesis at Cambridge University[1]. Information was collected from some 30 different firms of agents and comprised nearly 200 sales, all between 1988 and 1991. Only 13% of the acreage was sold as bare land, all sales were more than 50 acres and the sample was restricted to the four MAFF regions mentioned above. The value ascribed to houses in this survey is roughly 30%.

While it is possible to detect a bias towards residential sales in a firm of Savills' standing, the conclusion from these three sources of information must be that the value of the house is supremely

---

1 Long, NWL (1995) "The Non-Agricultural Influences on English Farmland Prices", unpublished DPhil Thesis, Cambridge.

important and this is hardly surprising. English people generally prefer to live in the country – and farmers regard the farmstead as a home as well as a place of work. They and their wives will increasingly continue to make the house a priority in their assessment of the value of a farm.

The agricultural factor

All the evidence over the years since Norton Trist & Gilbert wrote their letter, quoted at the outset of this chapter, seems to indicate that the agricultural quality of the land has had a diminishing influence on land prices. The evidence would seem to lie in Table 2 shown above. The reasons are not hard to find and are well epitomised in the table shown below.

Table 4 The diminishing relevance of output to land and other prices (with acknowledgement to Savills)

	1955	1989 Increase Decrease	Factor
Wheat price	£30 per tonne	£105 per tonne	x3.5
Average yield	1.35 tonnes per acre	2.7 tonnes per acre	x2
Average gross return for wheat	£40 per acre	£283 per acre	x7
Land price	£75 per acre	£2,600 per acre	x34
1 acre cost the average return of	1.8 acres	9.1 acres	x5
A man's weekly wage was met by the average return of	£7	£122	x14
	0.1 acre	0.42 acre	x4

The Centre for Agricultural Strategy, Reading, noted in 1993 that "Whilst farmland prices in England have fallen in real terms by over 20% [between 1978 and 1992] . . .real farm incomes have halved over this period".

The Cambridge research, referred to above, found that all the evidence from the inquiries pointed to the same conclusions. Data had been gathered on individual farmland sales from some 30 different firms of agents. Information was collected on nearly 200 sales, all between 1988-91. The results of this survey comprise the only dataset known to this writer which includes both individual farmland sale prices and a measure of the expected agricultural returns to those farms or blocks of land. This measure of agricultural returns was the rent or in cases where the property was sold with vacant possession, an estimated rent, which was or would have been paid by a sitting tenant.

The rent estimates from the sample were grouped into rental bands and Table 5 shows the mean prices per ha for vacant possession land in each band. As only about 10% of the acreage sold annually in the UK is tenanted, this analysis focused on vacant possession land. The prices are given in three columns, for land sold with housing, land sold with housing but with the house value subtracted and land sold as bare land.

Table 5 Per hectare price of vacant possession land by rental band

Rent level per acre	Land + house	Land − house	Bare land
£15–29	£5,560	£2,601	£3,243
£30–39	£8,027	£4,200	£4,257
£40–49	£7,055	£4,710	£3,576
£50–59	£9,844	£4,858	£3,266
£60–69	£11,236	£5,661	not significant
£70–85	£8,268	£7,825	not significant

Clearly the correlation between rent and price is much weaker in the first column than in the second. But even the figures in the second column suggest a very weak relationship at the £40–60 per acre rent level. The third column was based on a very small sample and appears to negate the theoretical land price/rent relationship altogether.

Faced with statistics like these it is not surprising that recent textbooks on valuation have tended to downplay the traditional theory that the price of land should equal the capitalised sum of its expected net returns. RG Williams's *Agricultural Valuations*[1] does not even mention it.

Nevertheless, there is still evidence to show that the quality of farmland should be a major determining factor in farmland prices.

---

1 Williams, RG (1991) *Agricultural Valuations* 2nd ed, Estates Gazette, London.

Table 6 below shows the extraordinary difference in gross margin and profit from land growing a 3.25 tonnes per acre crop of corn to that growing only 2.75 tonnes. The effect of set-aside payments has been omitted as these had very little impact on farming returns until very recently.

Table 6 Net return on growing winter wheat at varying yields on a farm of over 500 acres

Item		Grade III land Average yield of 2.76 tonnes		Grade III land Higher yield of 3.25 tonnes	
Sales feed wheat			£305		£360
Variable	Seed	£19		£19	
	Fertilisers	£26		£30	
	Sprays	£35		£41	
			£80		£80
GM			£225		£270
Overheads (Nix, Wye College) 1992			£225		£225
Profit			Nil		£45

The basic message is that it costs no less, often more, to grow corn on marginal land and it costs only marginally less to target a yield of 2.75 ha than 3.25 ha. The net financial result, however, can have devastating consequences.

The Cambridge research did pursue the "agricultural factor" and discerned a more precise relationship between price and returns, using a method of statistical analysis known as multiple regression. This procedure enables a researcher to disentangle the effects of several different factors, or variables, on a "dependent" variable, in this case per hectare land price (minus any housing value). A large number of factors were tested in various combinations using a statistical computing package, which found that the factors which were associated with ("explained") the most price variation were, in order of importance, agricultural rent, landscape quality, "rollover" relief and the acreage traded. This combination and its analysis are described at the end of the chapter.

As explained earlier, the Cambridge team used the selling agent's assessment of rent as the best guide to land quality available and found the figures for each variable very similar. Their analysis revealed a price variation for rent of 0.83 indicating that a 1%

increase in rent led to a 0.83 increase, on average, in land price. So they succeeded in isolating the agricultural factor and showed that it did relate to rental value and, thus, indirectly to farmland quality and potential.

Other determinants of land value relating to the property

1 Development

Over the last 20 years, the possibility of development has been given as a major justification for holding farmland when the income from it has seemed derisorily small. It attracted development land tax which was introduced in 1976 and not repealed until well into the 1980s. Yet in Savills' sample, development potential accounted for no more than 1.7% of the total value and this is supported by the figures collected by the Cambridge research. It is possible that these figures do not tell the whole truth. Both the Savills and Cambridge research excluded sales of below 50 acres and bearing in mind that land with planning consent seldom exceeds 50 acres and is usually sold separately from the farm, it is not difficult to see how the picture could have become distorted.

2 Size of the transaction

The size of a transaction has been found to have a price-depressing effect in several studies of land prices in the USA (in which house values had been subtracted, as they have here). This size effect probably reflects the fact that many sales are to neighbouring farmers, who can spread their overheads on the newly purchased land and in general, the larger the sale, the smaller these economies of amalgamation will be. Cambridge collected information for each sale on whether or not the purchaser was a nearby landowner (or tenant farmer), intending to amalgamate the property with an existing holding. Of land with buildings, 41% of sales and 39% of the acreage fell into this category, while for bare land the proportions were 21% and 25%. This factor was tested in regression but did not appear to have any effect on price, which suggests that for nearly all land the price level is set by neighbouring farmers. Outsiders, who would not profit from economies of amalgamation, generally have to have additional reasons for outbidding the neighbours besides mere farm profits. The data shows this to be the case. There were few sales where the buyer was not either a nearby farmer, or primarily interested in the "residence", or had rollover relief; in fact only 13% did not fall into one of these categories. The average acreage of this 13% was fairly small and many of the purchases were just for keeping horses. Very few purchasers were buying simply because they wanted to get started in farming.

3 Sporting

Another possible determinant of value which is correlated with attractive countryside is sporting potential. Sport appeared to have negligible effect on price in the Cambridge data. Agents were asked to estimate a rental value for shooting or other sporting rights on each property, but a value was only given in 10% of cases and in only 4% of the whole sample did this value exceed £1.50 per acre. Even then these estimates were mostly potential values and if sporting rights had been let this might have interfered with farming operations. Some agents interviewed during the survey considered that the value of sporting would probably be included in the house price. Indeed, the value of the sporting on any but the larger and better known sporting estates is likely to be fairly marginal. The value of a farm for pheasant shooting will depend to a large extent on the woodland component sold with it. One of the great incentives encouraging farmers to plant small woods today is the realisation that they will enhance the shooting. It is, however, rarely that one finds very much woodland included in the sale of a farm. The reason may be that in the middle years of this century, when about 60% of all farmland was tenanted, the landlord normally reserved the sporting rights and woodland was seldom included in the tenancy. As these farms were sold over the years, often to existing tenants, it was natural that the woodland would remain estate property so long as there was any estate at all and when these estates were sold, as many were, odd parcels of woodland were lotted together and often sold to timber merchants, thus remaining separated from the farmland which surrounded them. At the same time, most farmers preferred to spend any available money they had on improving their farms rather than buying back odd blocks of woodland, often recently felled and requiring expensive replanting. There has never been the tradition in this country for farmers to regard woodland as an ancillary enterprise to their farming, except perhaps in the chestnut coppice areas of Kent and Sussex. So it is today that these smaller blocks of woodland, which could enhance the shooting on the farms, are often separately owned. There are of course some superb partridge shoots on larger farms, particularly in East Anglia, but here the stock of partridges shrank during and after the last war owing to more modern farming practices and only recently have reared birds begun to restore some value to these shoots.

In looking at the sporting potential in a farm for sale it is often necessary to see what sporting value those farms may have to offer adjoining shoots by providing gun stands to serve adjoining woodlands, or some partridge shooting as a subsidiary variant to the main shoot in the early weeks of the shooting season. While accepting that most farms are playing an ancillary role in an adjoining shoot, their value for shooting may be substantially enhanced by any small woods judiciously sited and, in the short term, by planting game strips. As, however, it is seldom that a shoot can afford to buy a farm to serve its needs, any increase in the sale value of a farm occasioned by the sporting potential is likely to reflect the added income or enjoyment the farmer may receive by co-operating with his neighbours.

There are other forms of sporting which are less traditional but can be profitable. They include such activities as paint balling, motorcycle scrambling, clay pigeon shooting and horse-riding which do not necessarily require planning permission. Most of these activities can be carried out using existing buildings, if any buildings are needed. The potential for such uses to be profitable will depend less on the nature of the farm and more on its proximity to centres of population. Paint balling will require 20–30 acres of mature or semi-mature woods; clay shooting will require a site adequately isolated from other dwellings; and motorcycle scrambling will normally require an owner to have very tolerant neighbours! Horse riding is very variable in its requirements which range from a long-distance course requiring headlands and some well-constructed jumps to a livery establishment making use of redundant boxes and sheds with the room for an all-weather exercising yard. Being leisure pursuits these enterprises are dependent on prosperity and full employment. The recent recession has shown how vulnerable such sources of income can be.

4 Farmbuildings

The value ascribed to farmbuildings is difficult to arrive at. While replacement costs could be immense, most valuers would reduce their estimates of value to allow for a degree of obsolescence and redundancy. Farmbuildings have never affected farm values as might have been expected. To some purchasers of a farm there may be positive advantages in starting again with new buildings. In many cases existing buildings have become redundant or their design does not meet the requirements of purchasers. (After all how seldom does the "fitted kitchen" of one family find favour with the next!) However, somewhere in the late 1970s the scene changed. The monastic tithe barn, seen as a liability for two generations, became an asset attracting the public to an architectural heritage which also housed a farm shop. Traditional buildings became objects of interest worthy of protection to the extent that planners even allowed them to be converted to dwellings and industrial premises. The recession of the 1990s took much of the value off these assets, but the fact remains that "Fixed Equipment" has taken on a new meaning in the eyes of those whose task it is to discover the latent value in a farm for sale. Looking to the future, the traditional use of fixed equipment for farming is increasingly circumscribed by the requirements of scale, of Health and Safety regulations and by new technology. There may yet come new complexes which are intended to cater for a group of farms and which are capable of processing farm produce to make it more saleable for an increasingly demanding and selective market.

Where farmbuildings are redundant or where there is a market for non-agricultural use, no valuer selling a farm will overlook the potential for development and if planning permission has already been obtained for, say, the conversion of a redundant building to a dwelling house, the building of houses in the farmstead or for the extraction of minerals, it is likely that such development will be individually valued and sold separately although a purchaser for the farm may be invited to buy such lots with the whole. It is the latent potential development value that is often difficult to assess but which can have an important overall effect on the price of the farm. Selling agents sometimes find that where development permission may be difficult to obtain, it is better to titillate the purchaser's appetite with suggestions rather than to apply for such development and have it refused. How to present this potential tests the skill of any agent. An application to develop or to change the use of some old buildings may trigger off unsought problems if, as a result of the planning officer's inspection, the buildings are subsequently listed and some hitherto unnoticed non-agricultural activities attract an enforcement notice or a valuation for rating. Moreover, even if the attempt to crystallise development is successful and a part of the farm sold, the effect on the rest of the property may be to reduce its value by more than the development was worth.

It is also worth remembering that while the sale of farmland with actual or potential value will still attract capital gains rollover and retirement relief for taxation purposes, should a change of use have already begun or should the agricultural use have patently ceased, such reliefs will be lost when the land is sold.

5 Landscape quality

The most striking result to have come out of the Cambridge survey is the influence it seems to attribute to landscape quality. It should be stressed that the sample is biased as compared with what we know from MAFF data of the generality of farmland sales. Houses comprised roughly 30% of the value of this sample (possibly more if the house values were systematically underestimated), compared with the MAFF estimate of 18% in the four regions in total (for 1990). Probably the other "residential" factor, namely landscape quality, should be scaled down by the same amount. Thus, the effect of a unit change in landscape quality, on average, across the four regions shown in Table 3, would be £288 per ha, meaning that the difference between land rated 1 and land rated 5 would be £1152 per ha.

There are precedents for this finding in studies of the land market in the USA. A Texan researcher, C Arden Pope III[1], claimed in the 1990s that only 25% of intercounty price variation in the Lone Star state was attributable to agricultural returns and the rest was accounted for by differences in "consumptive" use values (ie recreational and residential, including development potential). The dependent variable in his model included house prices. Because his study was not of individual farm prices but county averages he was able to explain nearly all the price variation. As long ago as 1957 another US researcher, Jefferies, was asking if cattle ranching in Arizona was not primarily a recreational activity. England may not have a Wild West but there seems no reason, in principle, why

---

1 Arden Pope III, C (1985) "Agricultural Productive and Consumptive Use Components of Rural Land Values in Texas", *American Journal of Agricultural Economics* 67(1): 81–86.

riding should not become more popular and more land be given over to equestrian use. The main element in consumptive values will be farmhouses and cottages. It is likely that the differential between the price of houses in the countryside and urban or suburban prices will increase, assuming no fundamental changes in the planning regime. As far as UK agriculture is concerned house prices are a shrinking asset as more and more houses are sold separately from the land. This will reduce their importance as a component of land values, although this effect on land prices will be offset to an extent by the increasing rarity of genuine farmhouses surrounded by their own land.

The generally high and apparently "uneconomic" level of land prices is partly explained by amalgamation demand and this is discussed later in this chapter. But the amenity factor still seems to be highly significant, judging by the Cambridge results, despite the fact that house prices have been subtracted in every case. The coefficient of 0.12 for the landscape quality variable indicates that on average land is worth £480 more per ha for every unit increase on the scale from 1-5. Several points should be borne in mind in interpreting this result. First, the sample tested was entirely of vacant possession land sales over 500 acres and predominantly of sales with houses (94 out of 154 cases). It may, therefore, have been biased. Leaving those points aside, the influence attributable to landscape may be dependent on other factors. A value for any housing was subtracted in each case, but in practice the agent may have underestimated the price the house would have made if sold with the view and surroundings on the farm, if he or she merely compared it with similar houses in the area and estimated the price largely on size and facilities. The shortfall in house price, dependent on view and surroundings, would then be subsumed in landscape quality. Even if the agent did make an accurate estimate of the price that a house of the same quality and in the same position would have fetched, it is possible that a "marriage value" exists for sales of houses with land which disappears when each is sold separately. This might arise if the owner not only enjoyed attractive surroundings but felt those surroundings were under his control, and this hypothetical marriage value would probably be correlated with landscape quality. The connection between landscape quality and housing is borne out by another regression equation, in which only sales without houses (64 in total) were tested. For this sample the landscape variable was less significant statistically (the t-ratio was only 2.9), although the coefficient was still almost as large. Many of the bare land sales in areas of attractive countryside were to purchasers whose main interests were non-agricultural (often keeping horses), but sometimes conservation for its own sake, according to the agents. Nevertheless, a suspicion remains that other factors might have exaggerated the importance of the landscape variable.

Commenting on a survey of farm sales occurring in 1990 and 1991, Savills were able to say that amenity value was reflected in the sale price: "It appears to range from about £100 per acre to £500 per acre. In 1991 the effect was limited to properties within easy reach of London, but in 1990 the effect was observed more widely"[1]. Presumably 1990 was before the worst of the recession hit house prices.

6 Other factors relevant to the property

There are a number of other factors which may have only a marginal influence in a statistical analysis but which every valuer knows can be absolutely crucial to a sale price in certain circumstances. An intrusive public footpath, a nearby gipsy encampment or the impending threat of a development can render a property almost unsaleable.

Certain factors dictated by the common European policy have only begun to be felt and are discussed at the end of this chapter where future trends are examined. Included in this subject must be those designations which restrict production but may offer other opportunities for income or even enjoyment of the property.

External determinants

Those external factors must now be examined which affect the market and over which the seller may have little control. It is essential to understand their nature because any untoward effect can sometimes be mitigated by the timing of the sale and the form in which the property is presented.

---

1 Savills (1992) "The Amenity and Conservation Value of Land", Savills Agricultural Research, London. A report for the Countryside Commission.

1 The motives and circumstances of the purchaser. Capital gains tax rollover relief

Cambridge found the data on rollover gave no conclusive answers since the agents interviewed were normally only able to say whether this source had funded some part of the purchase price, not how much. Nor were they able to say, in most cases, whether the rollover came from sales of land for development or as farmland (or other business assets). In the case of farmland sales there were probably few capital gains to roll over in this period, except perhaps where farmers were benefiting from sales of houses which were not their main residence. Nevertheless, where there are any capital gains to roll over the beneficiary of tax relief has to reinvest in business assets the entire proceeds of the sale which gave rise to those gains, so it is probable that many purchasers buying new farms having sold their old farm were described as using rollover. Buyers with enough rollover to fund a whole farm purchase would in theory have an incentive to bid up to 40% above the "going rate", if the alternative would be to lose that 40% in tax. But it seems unlikely that they would need to bid up that far unless they were in competition with other rollover buyers. Thus, the effect of the "rollover premium" on farmland prices will depend crucially on the number of rollover buyers in the market. Savills have shown that in 1988 33% of all transactions involved rollover money as a source of finance[1]. This fell to 20% in 1989 and subsequently fell lower still, indicating that the large development gains of the 1980s had dried up.

2 Purchasing to spread overheads

Some purchasers were, no doubt, seeking to spread their overheads and sought to make purchases of adjoining land under circumstances which put them in a position to be able to pay more than their rivals. Why this should be so can be explained by the example in Table 7.

That this is no theoretical matter is borne out by a survey carried out by the firm of chartered surveyors, Bidwells, of Cambridge reported in *Farming News* on February 24 1995. This showed that of the 140 farmers surveyed, on average farming 1,200 acres, over 80 per cent said they could manage an extra 350 acres and some

---

1 Savills Research 1989.

20 per cent thought they could contract between 1,000 and 2,000 additional acres without significant changes in their tackle.

Table 7 Spreading overheads

		£
500 acres of corn	Sales 500 x £300	150,000
	Direct costs 500 x £100	50,000
	Gross margin	100,000
	Overheads say @ £213	106,500
Loss		(6,000)
200 acres added to the farm		
So		
700 acres corn	Sales 700 x £300	210,000
	Direct costs 700 x £100	70,000
	Gross margin	140,000
	Overheads say @ £200	140,000
Loss		nil

NB (1) These figures include rent or if land owned, a very modest service charge on borrowing of around 6%.

(2) A farm organised for 500 acres could probably absorb an additional 200 acres with minimal increase in total overheads save for rent/service charge and overdraft interest and so the level of overheads overall per acre will fall as they have done here.

Indeed, the fortuitous chance of securing adjoining land which might not be on the market again for many years may have resulted in a purchaser paying more than he might otherwise have paid. There are instances where bare land has changed hands at prices per acre not far removed from those paid for farms complete with houses and cottages. Again "bare" land may have a high marriage value for amenity purposes to a residential houseowner whose property it surrounds and without which demand it might never have been offered on its own. For these reasons the market for bare land may be affected by so many factors and so profoundly affected, as to limit the value of such prices in trying to arrive at the value of this component land value.

3 The farm structure in the locality

Another factor, alluded to above, which may have been correlated with landscape quality, was the farm structure of each locality (ie whether it was an area of small or large farms). If there is greater demand for land, to buy or rent, in areas with many small and marginal farms and if the institutional framework within which rents are set means that rent levels fail to reflect this demand, this would presumably be reflected in land prices. Information on the farming structure of individual localities was not included in Cambridge data, but so often more attractive countryside is generally correlated with areas of smaller farms. The problem with this hypothesis is that one would expect any such effect to be counteracted by a lack of effective demand (ie ready cash) among farmers in less profitable areas. It is striking, looking at the Cambridge survey data, to note how nearly all of the land in the South West (usually rated 4 or 5 for its landscape) was sold either with houses or stables, or permission to build them, largely to "non-farmers". It may be that local farmers did not generally buy land in amounts of more than 50 acres, but still set a general price level for all sales and if outsiders could not match that level then properties would be sold in lots of less than 50 acres. It would be interesting to know how many "non-agricultural" purchasers buying whole farms, particularly in the West Country, intended to sell them off piecemeal. Although hard to prove, it does seem likely that some of the putative £480 per ha attributed in the equation to a unit change in landscape quality should actually be attributed to farming structure, ie greater pressure to expand among marginal farmers.

4 The supply market

Much of the residual price variation in the Cambridge survey could probably only be explained with information which it would be almost impossible to collect, such as the state of supply and demand in the locality of each sale. Some academic economists dismiss supply factors as irrelevant to the price of land on the grounds that the total supply is virtually fixed (ie new land is not being created) and price is, therefore, entirely demand-determined. They do not regard the number of transactions over a period, nationally or in a locality, as a useful supply measure. On the other hand, it does seem likely that if, for instance, a number of financial institutions, more sensitive than most landowners to agricultural returns, decide to sell up at the same time and if their holdings are concentrated in, say the Eastern Counties, this will tend to depress the price of good arable farms in that area. An equation which included this information in some form, if it were true, would probably explain more of the variation. However, the supply effect is lessened by the fact that the "marketing" of more land brings with it more neighbouring farmers and, hence, maintains this category of demand.

If the rent variable had been adjusted in each sale to reflect, not the profit to be expected from the property by the average potential tenant, but the profit expected by the successful bidder and the underbidder to the sale, this would also have improved the regression. Much must depend on the extent to which potential purchasers can spread their overheads in making a purchase.

A related point is that the market for farmland is often a very "thin" market, particularly where there is no attractive farmhouse and neighbours are the bidders with the most to gain from a purchase. In those circumstances the availability of funds to each individual bidder will be crucial. This factor must have become more important as land prices have fallen and bank managers less inclined to lend.

5 Taxation

It is this last factor which has received scant attention from writers on land values, possibly because tax is a highly specialised subject and also because its influence on values is almost impossible to measure. Nevertheless, its influence during the last 30 years may have been far more profound than is often realised and in examining the subject those agents who dealt in land, experiencing these factors at first hand and whose advice was often simultaneously sought by buyers, are left to speak for themselves where such comments are available.

The opportunities of enjoying personal benefit from tax allowable expenditure on the farm which in turn could enhance the value of a farm with vacant possession is referred to by Desmond Hampton of Cluttons writing in *Farmland Market* in 1974[1]:

Throughout the period land was bought mainly by private individuals, either for farming or because they felt it was less easy to tax than equities or other liquid securities. Buying land was felt to be justified on tax grounds rather than on its straight investment merits.

---

1 Hampton, D (1974) "Agricultural Valuers – the expert prophets", *Farmland Market*, August, Estates Gazette and Farmers Weekly, London.

The tax system has an even greater influence on the availability of land for forestry. When the top rate of income tax and investment income surcharge totalled 98% in the 1970s and 1980s the cost to a top rate taxpayer of planting land under Schedule D was 2p in the £. Small wonder that forestry investment companies purchased hill land at over £300 per acre while better grazing land lower down, on offer to farmers, remained unsold at that price.

Before leaving the taxation of income as a factor in land values, it is worth remembering that from 1974 to 1984 rents suffered an investment income surcharge of 15%, bringing the top rate of income tax to the 98% mentioned above. While by no means the most important factor affecting let land values, it was one more nail in the coffin of the tenanted sector and by contrast with the treatment of farming income, may have inflated the price of land unencumbered with a tenancy.

The tax treatment of the farmer who sold his land came into prominence with the introduction of capital gains tax in 1965. As many farmers were selling to realise a planning gain, the ability to take advantage of "rollover relief" and reinvest in farmland paying no gains tax was a considerable relief, but this clearly inflated the price of land generally. Some commentators see this factor as the trigger for the spectacular rise in farmland prices of 1972–3[1]:

The boom and slump of the early 1970s, which saw the 1971 average of £262 per acre rise to £757 in two years and fall back to £539 in another two, deserves more particular examination. Both the severity of the cycle and the values involved were unique in this previously conservative market.

Why did prices rise so rapidly? The initial spark for the boom was struck in other factors of the property market. Fortunes were being made in urban development or sheer speculation and there was money a-plenty to buy land with the benefit of planning permission or for which there was a good chance of obtaining it. Prices of up to £50,000 per acre were commonplace for sites and the roll-over provisions of capital gains tax were so drawn that only a year was allowed to reinvest these enormous sums if CGT was to be avoided. Not surprisingly, the farmer vendors of this valuable land bid up the prices of other farms to retain their capital untaxed, and this excessive supply of "funny money" soon convulsed a previously well-balanced market. And as prices rose those who had made profits in other sectors of business

1 Clayton, J and Maunder, A (1977) "A Quarter of a Century of Agricultural Land Valuers", *Farmland Market* August, Estates Gazette and Farmers Weekly, London.

saw a safe and appreciating home for their nest-egg, so that more funds poured in.

Land prices fell again in late 1973 and in 1974. Again government fiscal policy was seen as a cause. Bill Young, writing of "Healey's Squeeze" in August 1975[1], summarised the situation as follows:

. . . recent taxation alternations, as enacted in the Finance Act 1974, proposed in the White Paper and outlined in the Green Paper, must all have a depressing effect on values.

- The removal of roll-over relief from development value means that even if the property market recovers there will not be cash searching for a roll-over outlet.
- Removal of 45 per cent relief must discourage buyers and perhaps introduce sellers.
- The non-avoidable capital transfer tax must also increase sellers in the long term.
- Wealth tax, though deferred in its effect, does not appear to favour farmers. In the long-term it produces more need for cash which will increase sellers.

Tax gave the market a further twist to its tail when in 1976 some of the worst fears raised by the spectre of penal taxation by the new Government receded. The wealth tax was shelved and the severity of capital transfer tax eased by the Finance Act 1976. 50% relief was given to the full-time working farmer and 30% to owners of all other business assets including let land. Moreover, the three years of grace given for reinvestment of the proceeds of development gains made in the boom years of 1972-73 were running out and once again ready money was chasing a limited supply of land. Land prices rose again reaching new heights in the property boom of 1988–9, but a significant difference was becoming apparent. No longer was the price so closely related to farm income potential or to the grade of land being sold. Other non-agricultural factors were playing an increasingly important part. Investors were looking to recreational potential, diversification and alternative uses for the buildings. The character of the house counted more than ever. It was a period in which farms were lotted and sold. The land was

---

1 Young, B (1974) "Mr. Healey's squeeze", *Farmland Market* August, Estates Gazette and Farmers Weekly, London.

often bought by neighbouring farmers anxious to spread their overheads. The houses and convertible buildings met the demand from those sharing in the city boom to move in to the country. Other buildings met the needs of smaller businesses characteristic of the 1980s, far out of town sites, hopefully at lower rents and rates. In all this, farmland, although treated no differently from other businesses, by its composition and nature reacted uniquely. Christopher Johnson, Chief Economic Adviser to Lloyds Bank, writing in *Farmland Market* in February 1990[1] commenting on the resurgence of farmland values and the effect of rollover relief states:

The increase in the top rate of capital gains tax to 40% in the 1988 budget clearly raised the value of the relief.

The rumour that roll-over relief might be ended in the 1989 budget spurred such purchases; the relief was continued, but some restrictions were imposed. Roll-over relief explains not only the come-back of personal purchasers to the market, but at least part of the surge in land prices. However, some of the prices financed by roll-over relief have been out of line with those not so financed, which adds to the difficulty of measuring land price trends.

The capital gains to be rolled over are due to the huge increase in the price of land for housing development, especially in the south-east. This in its turn has been caused by the rise in house prices, and the scarcity of housing land arising out of planning constraints. In 1988, the average price of housing land in England and Wales was £472,000 per hectare, one hundred times the price of English vacant farmland. The price of land for industrial and commercial development was of the same order of magnitude.

According to estimates for earlier years, something like 0.1% of all farmland is sold for urban development each year. If it has recently been reaching a hundred times the price of farmland in agricultural use, then it is clear that development land sales may have given a 10% annual return on the UK farmland area, as much as the total return on farming.

Prices of farmland steadied in 1990 and Savills had no hesitation in ascribing this to a decline in rollover funds[2]. Their records showed that while in 1988 42% of land purchased was financed by rollover funds, this had dropped to 14% by the following year. Subsequent publications from the same source show it dropped

---

1 Johnson, C (1990) "Farmland as a Business Asset", *Farmland Market* February, Farmers Weekly, London.
2 "Agricultural Land Price Survey" (1990) Savills Research, London.

further to 8% by 1991.

It was estate duty that caused farmland to be described as a tax haven for the deathbed purchaser and indeed it was known as an avoidable tax. It was, therefore, surprising that it took the Labour Government 10 years to introduce, in 1975, capital transfer tax. These two taxes between them had done much to break up larger estates, but the effect on farmland was lessened by a 45% valuation relief on farmland, increased in 1975 to 50% for a full-time working farmer. Such relief was, however, limited to £250,000 or 1000 acres, whichever was the greater. This concession was in line with the tradition of all parties to favour businesses, particularly small businesses, and as a result farmland was seen as a good investment for tax planning purposes. Whether this increased demand to a sufficient extent to negate the relief can never be ascertained, but it probably went some way towards it.

With the introduction of 100% valuation relief for inheritance tax in 1992 – for agricultural land in hand – and the retention of rollover relief from capital gains tax, in spite of serious proposals over the years to abolish it, most landowners will probably admit that the capital tax treatment of landed property is unlikely to get much better. It should now be possible to transfer an estate across to the next generation free of inheritance tax by use of a potentially exempt transfer. Capital gains tax should be minimal, if not a minus quantity, on let land and can be rolled over on the home farm. Farm values might be expected to reflect this inheritance tax relief and so they yet may , but this is to overlook the sea-change that has occurred in our price support system. Common Agricultural Policy (CAP) proposals on set-aside and headage payments are still being amended and have changed the nature of farming policy so profoundly as to dwarf, for the moment, other factors which have influenced farm land values in the past.

The future

The shift in the Common Agricultural Policy from support based on output has yet to be fully realised. Dairy quotas which came in in 1984 were quantifiable and above all transferable, at a price, so that while it has been the intention of the EC to reduce milk production overall, enough farmers have gone out of production through retirement or inability to meet effluent disposal requirements to enable the remainder to replace quota cuts and remain in business. Set-aside for arable crops has, at least for the moment, provided corn farmers with an area subsidy regardless of production, thus narrowing the profit differential between land grades. More ominously, headage payments which can be removed by an outgoer, tenant or freeholder can leave a farm which was pasture in 1991 with no quota, no area payment and no stock subsidy. There may be left two categories of farms, those which can be farmed and those which virtually cannot! This in turn should narrow the price differential between grades of land blessed with subsidies, but widen the price between those farms with and those without subsidies. It is likely though that the political support for farmers in the EC will diminish and payments will be allowed to wither with inflation. At the time of writing some cereal producers probably could compete with North American farmers on the world market, but they would face increasing competition from low cost producers particularly in Australia, Argentina and Eastern Europe. If subsidies were withdrawn simultaneously world-wide, high cost production on marginal land in Europe and North America would have to end; this might just allow UK producers on better land to revert to current levels of return.

Of course, future trends in farm incomes, the CAP and land prices will be subject to innumerable factors about which it would be unwise to make predictions. It is probably safe to assume that environmental pressures will grow and farmers will be encouraged or coerced into more conservation measures. The degree of coercion used will of course make a difference to land values. In the longer term there is the faint hope that concern about global pollution will stimulate industrial use of crops or coppice for fuel or plastics. Plastics are currently a more viable use for crops than fuel, but the need to find a substitute for petroleum to make plastics is less urgent environmentally and will depend on the price of oil. At the time of writing oil prices would need to double before this use was economic. The House of Lords recently appointed a Select Committee on the subject of industrial uses for agricultural products, which reported, generally, in the negative.

There appear, therefore, to be left two diametrically opposed policies which the European Community may follow. The one will attempt to maintain the existing rural structure with family farms familiar to those who follow the saga of Ambridge. It is probably the route preferred by those who look out from the windows of their week-end country cottages, who will at the same time heartily object to paying the costs which ignoring the market incurs. The alternative is for those market forces, and that means world market forces, to prevail to the ultimate benefit of better farmers on better land. As environmental restrictions curtail their production and world prices decline, they will expand to spread their overheads and the taxpayer will have fewer farmers to compensate for the environmental benefits that will be required of the latter. Another less attractive side will be the amalgamation of farms on land still in production and the abandonment of those on poorer land and in the uplands which will be left to satisfy the demands of leisure or form a relatively cheap backdrop to those period farmhouses from which yeoman farmers once farmed the land.

CHAPTER 10

Planning for succession

Synopsis
Position of the land manager – Make-up of estate – Special factors
– Owner's needs – Family's needs – Pattern of assets – Reviews.

Introduction

Any estate, whether landed or not, which is privately owned, in whatever form, will not pass unmolested by the State following the death of the owner if its value exceeds the current nil rate band of whatever death duty is in existence at the time. However, the impact of capital taxation may be lessened by judicious and well-informed tax planning. This book is not concerned to discuss the avoidance of capital taxes as such whether they be simple or complex, but, being a book on aspects of land management and landownership, it may be appropriate to consider what function the manager of an estate, and in the present context especially an agricultural estate, can perform in the process of capital tax planning. Where does the land manager stand in the hierarchy of experts usually involved in planning for succession? The precise answer to this question depends upon the functions of the manager of the estate and upon the closeness of his relationship with the owner for whom he may be working. There are some agents whose knowledge of the estate, of the owner and of his family is considerable; there are others with less profound understanding because they have been told less or have sought out less or have been required to do less, whose knowledge is therefore somewhat limited but who can nevertheless carry out some part of the planning process without difficulty.

The position of the land manager

The land manager stands in a special position as far as knowledge of the make-up of the estate, its lessees and tenants are concerned, for he is dealing with them constantly in the course of his daily work and will, over time, have come to know and understand many of them well. He is, therefore, in the position of being able to present a fairly detailed description of the estate and of those who live and work upon it. He has also a close knowledge and understanding of the current management process and of how it is likely to be affected by any proposed changes in the ownership structure.

Before any planning can begin it is essential that precise information is available on the constitution and jigsaw pattern of the estate. This pattern is likely to be broken, may indeed have to be broken, by the implementation of a tax-mitigation plan; particularly so where portions of the estate are, as under current law, granted special status in the matter of valuation for taxation. For example, over many years under estate duty, capital transfer tax and inheritance tax, farming and forestry land and businesses have, to a greater or lesser degree, been privileged in the matter of how the value ascribed to them on the death of the owner should be assessed, as indeed many businesses are now. Furthermore, so-called heritage property – land, buildings and works of art – may be specially treated. The tax planning team needs to know what assets forming part of the estate have or may have such status. The land manager, with his special knowledge should prepare schedules and plans showing the make-up of the estate under the following heads (or more or less as may be appropriate):

Farms
Tenanted.	Size. Composition. Tenants.
In hand.	Size. Composition.
	Farmed by owner.
	Partnerships.
	Share farming arrangements.
	Contract farming arrangements.

    Vacant or being vacated. Size. Composition. Present proposals
        for.
Commercial woodlands
        Size. Composition. Cottages.
Estate run businesses (other than farming)
        Details. Composition.
Mansion house and gardens
        Description of. Staff cottages. Opinion of "Heritage"
        quality.
Development potential on estate

Let properties (other than farms) eg
>Houses and cottages. Commercial ventures, etc.

Management
>Staff. Houses and cottages occupied by.

Financial statement showing:
>Rents and costs on let properties.
>Management costs.
>Profitability (or otherwise) of estate businesses.
>Estimate of current capital values of properties.

Special factors

Reference should be made to any special factors known to the manager which are not apparent "on the ground" such as known (or even suspected) future moves by tenants and lessees of the estates. Some may, for example, be thinking of leaving, others of business expansion, others be pressing for members of their family to be allowed to take over a tenancy or to join them in business partnerships. Yet others may be especially helpful or indeed difficult. Any properties on the estate which are likely to depreciate in value over the coming years are worth recording for they are not, in the normal course of events, properties to be given away.

Needs

Planning for succession will almost certainly mean financial and material sacrifice on the part of the present owner and calls for willingness on his part to accept change. This is not easy. Before any plan can be prepared and certainly before it can be implemented it is necessary that the owner should indicate his preferences and decide, in open consultation with his family if that is possible, what he is prepared to give up and the minimum size of the resources in both income and capital terms with which he is prepared to be left. These figures, requirements, immovables, will almost certainly change as the planning goes on. It is possible that the land manager could be the first of the advisors to be involved in this particular process for he should know something of the owner's needs, likes and dislikes, preferences and inclinations and he could be the first stalking horse. Within each family there may be members whose needs (as opposed to wants) are paramount and they should be identified. Within a family there may be a tradition or requirement that the corpus of the estate goes to the eldest son. Perhaps the land manager can tease out these sort of factors and examine them with the owner. If at any rate something of what the owner is prepared to accept as fulfilling his needs can be assessed then the process of tax planning, which will almost certainly involve re-allocating the estate assets, can begin.

There should now be a pattern of the assets, the resources, of the estate and beside it a note of the family needs, starting with the current owner and continuing through needs to wants and eventually perhaps to mere surprises. There may be a number of ways of meeting these needs, many patterns which the estate may take, many devices which the planners may suggest in the light of the law current at the time: these may impinge upon management and make the process easier or more difficult, more expensive or cheaper.

In planning for succession it must be acknowledged that the abilities and inclinations of the various possible beneficiaries cannot be ignored. An estate held by a number of different people (unless in some very tightly controlled form) may be broken to destruction in the long run. This is always a factor to be taken into account and is sometimes a significant one.

Reviews

Whatever the plan and however soundly based, it must be periodically reviewed. Often the whole process of implementation may be planned as a series of moves over the years during the course of which a death in the wrong order may throw things awry. Changes in the plan will be made as the law changes (as it will), as circumstances alter and as the generations grow and succeed one another, but somewhere at the heart must lie the intention to preserve the estate as a living entity. Should that intention waver the whole process is altered, the landholding degenerates to a mere investment for which tax planning is perhaps still necessary, but from which the heart has been torn. Then indeed "Golden lads and lasses must, like chimney sweepers, come to dust".

CHAPTER 11

Management objectives

Synopsis

Management objectives – Need for them – Unexpressed objectives
– Constraints – Long- and short-term objectives – Need for thought
– Estate Plan – Short- and medium-term – Budgets – Standards of
performance – Management report

Introduction

The management of any landed estate whatever its size or
constitution is an involved undertaking: the bigger the landholding
and the more extensive the structure of ownership the more
complex management becomes. Nevertheless, the thought that
objectives of management should be discussed and recorded in fair
detail is not often acted upon. That the management organisation
should know what it is trying to do is not a novel idea, nor is it
strange that the owner of a large landholding – which has for many
years been called a business – should consider from time to time
both what he or she wants of the estate and how that might be
achieved. When first thought about, a management objective may
appear so obvious that it does not need defining, being simply to
keep the estate functioning to the best possible advantage and to
hand it on as intact as possible down the generations of the family;
but when an objective is actually to be defined as opposed to
accepting that there is one which has never been expressed,
questions demand answers.

To run the estate to the best advantage must, of course, be an
objective even if it has never been voiced, but there are many
people involved in the estate and the "best advantage" of one is
not necessarily the best advantage of another. Actions, for example,
which will benefit the present owner may harm a successor; actions
which appear to benefit a successor or the present owner may
cause harm to those with lesser interests in the estate, the tenants
and lessees for example, which could in turn ultimately rebound on

the freeholder. It must not be forgotten that in letting lands the owner has dispersed his rights and, in the process of management, those rights which have been passed over to third parties must be maintained.

Unexpressed objectives

When an objective is outwardly expressed, even if it is a simple and obvious one, questions at once emerge. If no objectives are formulated questions do not come to the forefront of the mind and will only arise when a management decision is called for, and there is no certainty that the decision made will link to any previous decision, nor be remembered when a future choice presents itself. Management in this unsure state would appear to be by instinctive "feel", influenced, of course, by what the manager or owner thinks is right at the time because each is acting in accordance with unexpressed objectives, which have in fact never been discussed. Taken a step further such management is comfortably inactive until an unexpected crisis erupts when it will tend to react spontaneously. It is a fact that the management of any business is faced from time to time with emergencies of greater or lesser import. Such events can be dealt with more easily if there is in view a management objective than if each one is allowed to have its individual and unalloyed impact.

Constraints

When objectives are defined positive thought can be given to methods by which they may, perhaps, be achieved and this should also be the time to think about constraints, namely actions which will not be taken to attain an objective (there are often many). Some of the constraints will be set by the landowner, some by the management team and some by statute. Various constraints proposed may be argued about and in the course of time may be removed or modified; others will appear immutable. Constraints should be as few as possible and defined as ways in which management is not to act. Objections to proposals seem to come naturally when the proposals are made. These are not the same as predefined constraints.

Short and long term

The main land management objective is long-term, but there are also medium-term and short-term objectives. A long-term objective should be set out as simply and succinctly as possible, telling what it is that management is required to achieve. This will not necessarily be to a fixed time scale. In many cases it will be no more than "to maintain the landholding in such a way and in such a form as may be expected to ensure its survival for the benefit of the owner, his immediate family and those whose livelihoods depend upon it". In an example such as this it may have to be accepted that the survival of the whole is not possible, in which case the core of the estate, that to be retained to the last, should be identified.

Where the landowner is an institution or some form of trust or charity the prime objective may well be defined in the resolution or document setting it up. For management use such an objective may need to be enlarged.

Why?

When an objective has been set it will be helpful and mind-opening to ask "Why?". What is the reason for the particular objective chosen? In the case of a private owner where an objective has been stated as being to provide for himself and his family, without qualification, then it could be reasonable to suggest that a landholding is not necessarily the best vehicle by means of which the stated objective can be achieved; so it is right to ask, "Why?". The answer to the question "Why?" will often be subjective, being one based, and understandably based, on attachment to the land, on family feeling, on nostalgia or just, as suggested in a previous chapter, on the magnetism of territory (which encompasses all three).

Working plan

Aiming at this long-term objective and bearing in mind, if they are indeed expressed, the reasons behind it, the land manager may then produce a working plan with some sort of time-scale and with some dated proposals. The path chosen will twist and turn and there will probably be more than one path available. Different managers may have different methods and approaches, as may different owners, so that when managers change, the path may change to a greater or lesser extent, but the objective remains unaltered. As a policy is formulated constraints will arise – actions which, in the furthering of the plans, the owner or his advisers are not prepared or not able to take. Where constraints have been identified, discussed and agreed they should be made specific. Other constraints or obstacles will, of course, appear from time to time; some of them, perhaps unexpectedly, placed there by legislation. A change of government is often the occasion on which new constraints on action are set up, but it may also be an occasion on which old obstacles are removed. Obstacles placed by statute, or those removed, may well cause a change of policy without changing the objectives towards which that policy is directed. For example, this may happen when taxation alters or landlord and tenant law is changed.

Long-term objectives by their very nature should not be the subject of frequent alteration. There will be occasions on which they need reviewing and possibly modifying, but fundamental change in objectives could disrupt policy and set management into confusion. The only obvious occasion for a serious review of long-term objectives is on a change of ownership whether through gift, inheritance or purchase.

Estate ownership structure today is sometimes complex. What may appear to the outsider to be a single estate in the hands of one owner is often in fact a landholding in the ownership of a variety of different people or trusts with different trustees and different beneficiaries or indeed of a number of separate family companies. Usually such ownership holdings are managed as one and the objectives of each ownership unit are the same, or at least very similar, and the "head of the family" is in effective control of the lot.

It must be appreciated that since time does not stand still and since persons and personalities change, a long term objective will not, in the long term, be reached, but it may remain a moving light towards which management is required to steer.

A landed estate usually consists of a number of different departments or enterprises for which objectives may be set for the medium term (say five years). The ownership sector must not be left out of medium-term planning, for it is likely to be more efficiently managed and administered if within its long-term objectives successive medium-term and short-term plans are made.

Medium term

A medium-term plan for the ownership department might be for the next five years and be to some extent a rolling one. The implementation of this plan is a step on the route to be followed towards the long-term objective. It will contain practical management proposals for action within the reasonably foreseeable future and will move towards the moment when they can be implemented. That this moment may never actually arrive must be accepted, for circumstances can alter quickly: this, however, is no reason for not thinking ahead. Ownership department medium-term plans can and perhaps should be less detailed than those prepared for the future running of an active business such as a farm or other entrepreneurial venture, but to leave tomorrow alone to take care of itself is not asset management; it is crisis management. That there will be crises, that the unexpected will happen, must be accepted – indeed it is one of the excitements of management – but an estate which moves forward under some degree of planned control must leave management less prone to make mistakes than one on which action takes place only as a reaction to events.

Budgets

All businesses budget and plan for the future and estate enterprises are, or should be, no exception, for it is essential to realise that landownership is as much a business as is land occupation and must be treated as one. There is, however, a further complication in that estate trading concerns, farming, forestry, recreational ventures, etc are part of the whole and contribute to or detract from it. Budgets and plans for each sector must be prepared with an eye on the complete picture and must be seen as steps along the path over which the long-term objective is approached. They should not compete with each other except in so far as competition stimulates, rather than deadens, action.

Standards of performance

The allocation of resources between the different departments of the estate is not simple. How much, over the year, or some other period, should be put into one sector or another? How much withdrawn? Resources are finite. What is the measure of need? Standards of performance as applied to business ventures are useful gauges when comparing one sector of the estate with another, but they must be used with perception. The universal measure, return on investment, is not easily applied to some estate enterprises, not least because the extent of the investment is sometimes difficult, if not impossible, to calculate. However, mere difficulty should not be allowed to stand in the way. From the point of view of estate ownership, return on landed capital, evidenced by the ratio of net rental income to capital value, requires a realistic assessment of current values – a lengthy and often expensive undertaking which may call for the application of an agreed convention – and the assessment of a market rent for all estate properties which are not currently let (probably omitting the owner-occupied mansion house from both calculations).

Return on investment on trading enterprises should not be difficult to arrive at from an intelligent study of the accounts, providing of course that there is a reliable record of the resources put into and used by them. Within the estate context, however, there is often more than return on investment to take into account. The in-hand farm, for example, as a single-proprietor business, as a partnership or other joint venture may have been established not only to generate income but also, and perhaps even primarily, as a means through which savings in capital taxation may be effected so that at least some portion of the estate may be passed on. The woodlands, often a source of income loss, may also be run as a commercial venture but with the same prime objective in view, namely estate preservation. In any event, if the estate is to be retained it must be used by somebody if for no other reason than to fulfil the owner's obligations to the community at large to cherish and maintain the countryside. So, as a measure of the right to a claim on estate resources, return on capital is not necessarily a simple instrument of management. This statement should not be read as an excuse to ignore measures of performance on the various estate enterprises. Owner and manager must be aware of the implications of performance as a base from which to consider future action and the allocation of resources but, in so doing, must accept that there are a number of items, largely immeasurable in money terms, to be thrown into the balance.

"Return on investment" as a measure of the performance of the ownership department presupposes that the current market value of the estate is known and this is almost certainly not the case unless the property has been very recently purchased. To set up such a record it is necessary to adopt some conventions or rules which will take account of such records as the estate may possess and alter them when recorded changes take place. For example, a starting-point could be the last time at which a "proper" valuation took place such as on the occasion of a death, the setting up of a trust or when a purchase or sale takes place. In between times the "historic" value is carried forward, altered as necessary by known capital changes until the next full revaluation.

Objectives, long-term or medium-term, and plans for the future are of little use unless their implementation is regularly examined. The consequences of each year's working should be set out and commented on. The results of the year's trading may seem to be apparent from a perusal of the annual accounts, but if that examination is no more profound than a quick glance at the surplus or deficit, the profit or loss, most of the work will have been in vain. What has happened in the past is a guide to the future, so how a job has been done needs to be examined and explained.

Examination of results

To assist the owner and to help management it is essential that when the annual accounts are being presented to show the results of both ownership and occupation, a report is prepared commenting upon them, comparing them with previous years and, thus, examining the various sectors of the whole estate. It is not unoriginal to suggest that the separate enterprises of the in-hand farm are detailed and their contribution to the total farm profit or loss assessed and it should be accepted that a similar analysis of the accounts of all the other estate enterprises must be presented, for such analyses are an effective management tool. Here the ownership side must not be forgotten. A comparison of the year's results with those of the previous year is a useful and sometimes disturbing activity. What has changed between the two years? Why have repairs to property cost so much? What, over the years, has been the ratio of maintenance costs to rental income? What was it in the year under review? What of the ratio of management costs to income? Is it right? Does it seem to be too much or, indeed, too little? Where is the whole enterprise heading and why? Alterations in the estate itself should also be reported and if necessary commented upon. What sales or purchases have taken place, why and at what price? Has the structure of ownership been in any way altered? How and for what reason?

An estate report of this nature has at least three particular advantages. First, the preparation of it is in itself an excellent management discipline. Second, it gives the landowner a positive and sharply focused picture of the financial standing of the estate, of the processes of management and of progress or regress, success or failure, of the different sectors of the estate over the year and, third, it can show how far objectives are being realised. Yearly reports are also an invaluable historical record of the path trodden and, often, of the reasons behind decisions taken and acted upon.

A management report at the end of the year should be based on more than an analysis of the accounts, for today landownership, like farming, must explain itself and action taken or planned to enhance or protect the appearance of the countryside, to subscribe to, as well as control, public access, to improve the lives and fortunes of the local inhabitants, should not be concealed, however repellent the idea may at first seem. If landownership is ever to be accepted by the nation at large and especially by the inhabitants of any particular area of the managed countryside its actions must be made known.

Some estates, particularly the larger ones, have an "open day" from time to time when the opportunity is taken to demonstrate to the visiting public of what the estate consists, its own trading enterprises such as farming and forestry, its let lands and its contribution in terms of goods and services to both national and local well-being.

There is every reason why such a practice should be extended to the smaller estates in any given area which might work together to demonstrate to the public the contribution which they collectively and individually make to the general welfare: such demonstration should ideally include let farms and businesses on the estate. It is no doubt easy to make this suggestion and difficult to put it into practice, but co-operation between organisations which represent landowners and farmers might produce a workable scheme and could do great good.

CHAPTER 12

Conclusions

Synopsis
Decisions out of time – Threat to ownership – Place of public –
Government control – Change – Place of landowner

Decisions out of time

This book has not tried to address all aspects of landownership: it
has instead sought to follow certain paths to a central core, namely
management.

Ownership of any productive or important asset must, in making
its executive decisions, look to the future. Many actions of
management do not have an immediate result and decisions have
to be made in the light of what is intended to be their ultimate
effect: they are usually based on a knowledge of the facts at the
time and on past experience. However, the facts at the time evolved
from the past so that, indeed, most decisions are made in the glow
of the sunset rather than in the brightness of the sunrise. Astute
management decisions should be made in anticipation of the future
rather than in memory of the past. Would that this were possible.
Mankind lives in an ever-changing world and at the end of the 20th
century the countryside is changing very fast indeed.

The threat to ownership

The ownership of rural property, particularly of the large landed
estate, has been under threat for the last 100 years at the least, but
not entirely convincingly. Private agricultural estates have
diminished in number and size since the beginning of the century,
yet at the same time new ownerships have come into being, both
individual and institutional. Some take up ownership with the
intention of enjoying what they see as still being its social benefits,
some do so with altruistic motives, some with an eye on what has
proved over the longish term to have been a sound investment,

some with the hope and intention of making a capital gain as soon as possible.

The threat to the private ownership of an estate in land may develop and grow or it may lessen in the immediate future, just as it has grown and lessened since 1945. Whether or not there is a threat of extinction (and a policy of getting rid of the private owner is of course a political decision) it has to be accepted that public attitudes to such ownership, particularly of rural land, have changed markedly over the second half of the 20th century. This change has taken place partly perhaps because the importance of the land of this country as the producer of much needed food seems to the public to have declined; partly because the public has not yet become aware of the enormous potential of the land to produce crops for other than immediate human or animal consumption, nor of a potential resurgence of demand or food, but mainly because a much more mobile population has become aware of the countryside and has recognised its attractions; such recognition has been reinforced by the appointment of such bodies as the Countryside Commissions. The demand for and the chance to take recreation in the countryside has increased. In addition, many people now want to live in rural surroundings and when they do, have no wish to forego the amenities of urban life it they can help it.

The concern of the public

Concern for the countryside has resulted in a real desire by many to gain access to the rural world (sometimes a world of their imagination) and to have a say in its preservation and use. This desire is not going to fade; indeed it is sometimes not just a desire, it is near to determination.

The "this land is our land" attitude cannot be dismissed. Indeed, it may be supported where it claims not ownership of the land (whatever that may be) but ownership of rights to enjoy the land, the landscape, the countryside for which millions over the years have fought. An owner may understandably resent claims that others have rights over his land, some of which have no legal recognition; these claims may range from accepted rights of public passage to unacceptable claims for free public access or to dictate details of land use. Control over development is acceded to, though often fought against, but it must be acknowledged that such controls will grow under the pressure of public opinion. Where in the past the landowner has often held a commanding position and the ineffectual public a weak one, the tables may in the future be turned in that public demand for control will be so strong that the farmer and the landowner will need protection against it.

Government control

Government has, of course, over many years appreciated that there is, in the public interest, a right and obligation to regulate commercial and personal relationships, for mankind is not perfect and does not always treat his fellows well, so that certain controls have been necessary (in the sphere of landlord and tenant for example). These have been imposed and lessened and changed and bent, approved of and disapproved of and, being there, have inevitably affected the management of property.

They have influenced an owner's willingness to grant tenancies and leases of commercial and domestic property. They are there partly because the more powerful partner has been in a position to exploit, in a pejorative sense, the weaker. The difficulty about controls, however necessary they may be, is that they often result not just in acceptance but also in rejection and reaction which negates their primary aims.

Will future demand force government to take greater control than it now has over the use and management of land? Will the pressures, briefly mentioned above, result in the grant to the public of greater access to larger areas of rural land? Will public insistence persuade the legislature to impose positive planning on the countryside? Will farmers' commercial judgment as to how to use their land for farming be proscribed further? If it is, then to whose true benefit would this be?

Some new residents in the countryside (and some old too) object that certain of the smells and sights of farming are not only noxious but worse, depreciate the value of their property. They have sometimes a valid claim for consideration. How much further should such claims be supported?

Who is responsible?

Public awareness that the landowner is essentially a different person from the farmer (even when he is the same individual) is strangely dim. The farmer, the actual occupier of land, tends to be held solely responsible for how the countryside is used and is thought of as being the owner (which of course he often is). When the landowner is blamed for what some consider to be misuse of the land he is usually blamed as farmer rather than as owner; yet despite the freedom which the tenant farmer enjoys to farm in his own way, the owner as landlord can still exercise some control over the use and care of his land as far as the law will allow him.

Management must look to these matters in making its decisions and must accept that the clock is not going to be put back, accept that the public will have more rights over land in the future and that control is more likely to grown than diminish.

Taxation of course, and capital taxation in particular, has a profound influence on the workings of commerce and industry. Estate duty as overtaken by capital transfer tax and by its weaker offspring inheritance tax, have between them had a significant influence on the management of property and particularly of rural estates. A change in the structure of capital taxation, experienced, expected or feared, will alter the actions of management and in some cases will negate entirely what has already been done.

Farming change

Technical and scientific developments in farming, the growth and decline of financial support from government, quotas and other attempts to control production and the possibility in the future that European agriculture may have to function in a free market are all altering the structure of farming and of farms themselves. The small farm in Britain, particularly in the eastern counties, has almost ceased to exist. In the hills of the west the future is uncertain. Farming in the free market may in some areas become an unprofitable exercise. Estates will have to look to the future of their lands, to the structure of their farms, to the possibility of a depopulated countryside and will have to consider with care what, if anything, they can do about it. Will present policies allow them to do nothing or virtually nothing? Rural life may not in the future be sure of being able to depend upon the prosperity of agriculture. Other enterprises may have to be introduced and accepted. On the other hand, a growing world population may steadily increase the demand for food and, thus, turn policies and predictions upside down.

The place of the landowner

Many landowners today look upon themselves as guardians of the countryside, working both with and against the various authorities and bodies which seek to control their actions (for the public is not always right). Some could do more to bring the public on their side. Government, national and local, can act only through their servants who, as individuals, have opinions and prejudices like everybody else and are as prone to make mistakes. It is suggested that without the landowners, especially those who have a deep sense of the responsibilities which rest upon them, the countryside would be worse served than it is. This is a suggestion which some people will greet with smouldering disbelief; but what do they want? Do they want public control through bureaucracy and the official in place of the individual? After all, the individual resident owner is there in person to answer criticisms, to accept or reject suggestions, to act, as far as the law will permit, on his own behalf.

It must not be forgotten that the public have certain rights over land and that these must be respected. The danger is of over-respect on the one hand and over-claim on the other. In essence "this land is our land". "We" are both owner and public and there should be no rivalry.

Conclusion

Is there a danger that future regulation, future action and intrusion will lessen the compulsive will of owners and of occupiers too, to preserve their estates. Some, of course, may think that this would be a good thing: thoughts which may arise from some degree of jealousy but which also arise from a misunderstanding of the countryside and its structure. A misunderstanding of the essential commitment of the dedicated landowner. A misunderstanding which sometimes senses only a proud disdain?

The personal power of the landowner has waned and in its stead is growing the outlook of a new generation; one which must be persuaded, if necessary, to acknowledge the inheritance of a burden of responsibility which can be a joy to accept in the uncertain times which lie ahead.